# From the
# Palace to Prison

## Gary Armstrong

## New Wine Press

New Wine Press
P.O. Box 17
Chichester PO20 6YB
England

Names have been changed for various reasons.

Short extracts may be used for review purposes.

Bible references are from the Authorised Version.

ISBN 0 947852 84 0

Typeset by The Ikthos Studios, Chute, Andover,
Hampshire, SP11 9DS.
Printed in England by Clays Ltd, St Ives plc.

# Dedication

This book is dedicated to those who, by reason of their love and support, have brought it into being. My wife Roberta, daughters Michelle, Adelle, Danielle, Naomi and my boy – Aaron.

Also to the longsuffering people of Ulster, Catholic and Protestant, who will find true unity only in the Lord Jesus.

And most of all to the Lord Jesus whose love, grace, beauty and salvation continue to overwhelm me and cause me to worship Him. HE IS ALTOGETHER LOVELY.

# Contents

# Foreword

It was a Sunday night after our gospel service. There was a knock at the front door. When I opened the door a young man was standing there. He wanted to know whether I was the pastor of the church next door. Having replied in the affirmative, I invited him in. The young man, of course, was Gary Armstrong. Thus began a friendship which continued during his seven years with us at Emmanuel church, and continues to this day. Gary had just moved into the area of Northwich. He was concerned to find a suitable spiritual home for the family. Gary and Roberta intended to stay in the area for about three years. However, they quickly became an integral part of God's family at Emmanuel. The work became their work. Gary was a modern example of the verse *"The zeal of thine house hath eaten me up."* (John 2:17)

Gary's commitment and enthusiasm for the Lord was an example to everyone. During his time with us Gary was appointed a Deacon and Church Secretary. Later he was nominated as an Elder. He fulfilled these duties as unto the Lord. Gary was clear in his convictions. He was sometimes controversial, but his obvious love for the Lord and concern for God's glory helped offset this. If you could not always take to what he said – and sometimes how he said it! – you could not help but take to the man.

The testimony you are about to read was known by only a few at Emmanuel Church. I commend Gary's testimony to you as further evidence of the greatness of God's grace. Again the Lord demonstrates that nothing is too hard for him. I pray that as the 'Gary Armstrong Story' reaches a wider public, God will be glorified, for the end of all things is the glory of God. (Romans 16:27, 1 Corinthians 1:31)

Pastor Barry Cunningham
Emmanuel Evangelical Church,
Old Hall Road,
Northwich, Cheshire.

# PART I

## Chapter 1

# Strange Surroundings for Young Gary

Lying on my back, I looked up – two of the twelve little square panes were missing; a cold December air pierced the aired cell and I realised for the first time that I was in terrible trouble. The things that had promised me satisfaction had brought me emptiness; the pursuits that had promised happiness had brought misery and my self-erected honour had brought me disgrace. From my prison cell in 'D' Wing amidst the hubbub and confusion of a politically charged melting pot, I reflected on a life now reaping the harvest of many scattered seeds.

I was born in No. 8 Orlit Cottages, Ballinagallia, Armagh on 2nd June 1954. Before I left my mother's womb I was inheriting more than my parents genetic features – I was being brought into a fiercely staunch Protestant home with working class parents who proved to be the victims of their own weakness. Times were hard and not made easier by my parents' failure to get their priorities right. They, as young parents, loved a good time. How well I remember Friday nights – 7pm my mother put on her best dress and struggled with her hair, as my father changed into his best coat and trousers, and put on his Brylcreem. Off they went – either for the bus some miles away, later on on his old motorbike, and years later in a car. (Sometimes we were left to our own devices, and that was usually the signal for brotherly love to give way to unilateral declarations of war.)

Our home was poorly furnished and the regular arguments of my parents, coupled with the reckless adventures of energetic boys, ensured that at least one window in the house was boarded up. We always had dogs and cats who spent some of their time in our beds, secretly smuggled in. Anything from blind "Bruno" the greyhound (my father bought him as a pedigree in a pub and the first day I took him excitedly to hunt, his poor vision prevented him from seeing a hare run past him and his smell only enabled him to run straight into the hedge in pursuit), to three legged "Jet," the little Cairn who lost a leg in a revenge attack by our neighbour. We had a very large garden but it grew wild most years and must have caused our green-fingered neighbours, already hard pressed to contain our wayward and wild family exploits, much annoyance.

The moderating and refining influence in this unsavoury debacle of careless, unfettered family growth was that of my grandparents Robert and Florence Johnston. Their farm adjoined our back garden – three minutes across two fields and up one, brought us into the farmyard – there we spent much of our youth, helping and hindering but ever being nourished, cherished and loved. There we were fed when hungry, comforted when lonely and occupied when idle. My grandparents were regular Church attenders and I was always dreading Sunday morning, as I would look out my bedroom windows to see if XZ 7087, the Austin Seven, was at the front of my grandparents home. If it was it meant we had to go to Church. I certainly did not want to go out and tell my grandmother, "I'm not going" – for when I did the reception was much akin to "frosty contempt". I hated Church and although I went to Sunday School occasionally and the Boys Brigade occasionally, I could never get used to associating with the "townies". In Church I would make up football teams with hymnwriter's names – Banks, Wilson etc., and always loved those ministerial words, "Let us pray" – it was over!

We were indebted to our grandparents as boys for the only holiday we ever got – to Kilkeel with our grandmother, and also for day's outings. Sunday School trips accounted for other ventures. My only abiding memory of these was the day I ran across the road in front

11

of a police motorcyclist. I didn't wait to hear the lecture he gave my mother on my behalf – I COULD HAVE BEEN KILLED! My grandmother was the worst driver ever to put a foot on an accelerator and a hand on the gear stick, neither of which she ever did in synchronisation. She rarely stopped at 'T' junctions for she never touched second gear and the fact that she never had an accident until very late in her life bears more witness to providence than professionalism. We loved them both and in many ways they were more parents to us than our own parents, as grandparents often are. They had passed the stage of early thirties flirting and flitting – their maturity merely emphasised my parents' immaturity – their wisdom my parents' folly. Little was I to realise that what I was seeing early on as the failures in my parents were too soon to be evidenced in my own life.

In 1967 with the Civil Rights marches and growing sectarian strife I was well on my way to a Grammar School education, having passed my eleven plus with such good results as to warrant my mother being overcome with delight and sending me to the Royal School Armagh at great expense and not a little hardship. I was to regret that decision many times in my education as I struggled to buy books, uniform, slippers etc. I will never forget the jibes and mockery aimed at me by the 'snobs' and rich men's sons as I arrived in school to put on my mother's slippers to wear on the new school floors – (my parents couldn't afford to buy me any) – or the occasions I had to go to the Bursar's office to pay as much as my parents could afford of a growing school fees bill. It was one thing to send their son to the Royal School – another to pay his way there and I was always self-conscious of our comparative poverty to the affluence of others. I would never invite my friends home. I could never go on trips with them and all the time I sought to disguise what must have been embarrassingly apparent to all, except schoolboys do not embarrass easily.

I had to fight to make a reputation and fight I did, earning the reputation of being a "hard man" – fighting older boys, younger boys and when necessary the teachers. Saturday mornings at school were my release – I could sneak into my parent's bedroom and rifle the pockets of my father's trousers or my mother's purse. They were lost to the world, recovering from the night before. I was never caught stealing and at times I took small fortunes only to blow most of it on sweets and chips with the boys. A real anomaly – threadbare trousers but lots of money for "garbage". We smoked, vandalised and ate our Saturday mornings away – our gang was feared by the boys in school and known by those outside. Everyone else joined the Army Cadets – we opted out and played football. We were notorious in class and out of it. I lost count of the canings, detentions and lines – I wouldn't conform, and in my non-conformity I found the power and satisfaction that I had lost as a result of my upbringing.

The troubles in Ulster grew worse but somehow I remained apart, spending most of my teenage years at home or with my grandparents. Even when violence exploded in Armagh and my father and brother were arrested and charged with disorderly behaviour for stoning the Roman Catholics, I remained detached. My father and brother were sentenced to six months in prison but on appeal had their sentences suspended. I was approaching my O Levels in an environment of sectarian hatred and educational rebellion. Eventually I passed six O Levels and decided to stay on at school to do History and French at A Level. Those two years were just one series of fights, and ever increasing rebellion against the school institution, the teachers and the snobbish brainboxes who seemed too learned to be human. Football matches and cricket matches also filled my time. This was the only honour I earned in school, and I was so proud to wear the purple jacket with white trim that distinguished me as a 1st X1 sportsman. (My grandmother bought it and I still have it). It all culminated in my decision to drive a tractor for my cousin on the days I was supposed to be doing my A Level exams. I had opted out and unknown to my parents had ditched the school and everyone else.

At seventeen I was leaving school, but worse still my search for macho recognition with girls had brought a 5"0', brown haired school athletics champion into my life. I never had much experience of girls, having failed to establish any steady girlfriends, and I suppose I was naive, as I fell in love and ran away from its uncontrolled consequences. This was a traumatic period for me – my grandfather had died in my arms some twelve months earlier, leaving me devastated and the one to carry on the responsibilities of the farm; the troubles were getting worse and my family's involvement more pronounced; I had failed to do my A Level exams, and I was unemployed; marriage beckoned; and I HAD JUST TURNED EIGHTEEN. To cap it all my grandmother had had an accident in the car, well overdue, but unbelievably not her fault! She was in hospital.

# Chapter 2

# A Policeman's Lot

In September 1972 I applied for and was accepted into the Royal Ulster Constabulary, who were at this time, in the wake of the disbanding of the "treasured" B. Specials, more and more in the front line. The I.R.A. had taken over the Civil Rights leadership role and sustained, lifetaking violence had superseded the stonethrowing and name calling. As I made my way to the depot at Enniskillen to join other recruits in a three month crash course I had no concept of how serious the situation was in Ulster and was even less conscious of the role I was to play in it.

My wife had our first baby, Michelle Anabelle Margaret Armstrong, and each weekend as I returned from the depot I would return to my parent's home, where we stayed, with a gift for my little daughter. Having applied myself to the training I did well at the depot, and came out after twelve weeks with a very good report. It wasn't long before I learned I was to be posted to Newtownhamilton on the South Armagh border. In late 1972 this raw, rough eighteen year old recruit arrived at one of the most vulnerable and marked police stations in Ulster. Yet I never gave it a second thought – I was proud to be a policeman and I felt I had a contribution to make in bringing the violence to an end. I could travel home easily and live with my family and I was part of a close knit and small team of policemen. I felt that I had really arrived, and on a wet Monday when I did, the army lookouts, the security barriers, the bullet-proof jackets and the machine guns did nothing to deter me.

I wasn't in Newtownhamilton many weeks when, with George and the Sergeant, we went to Cullyhanna to serve summonses. I knew it was a terrorist stronghold but whilst sitting in the back of the Landrover on the way back to Newtownhamilton, I was completely shocked when a burst of automatic gunfire exploded from the roadside and I clearly saw the bullets fall on the landrover floor, having hit the inside of the side of the landrover opposite to where I was sitting. I didn't freeze, I just didn't do anything. I just looked for the gunmen, but they had fired from, as it were, my side and I was looking in the wrong direction. By way of response I belatedly took cover. When we got back to the station we examined ourselves and the landrover – several Thompson sub machine gun rounds had hit the inside of the Landrover, one had passed through the front window between George driving, and the skipper in the front passenger seat. As I drove home that night

I was overwhelmed by two thoughts – I had been in action with terrorists and I HAD ESCAPED!

I was relatively unaffected as I mixed conventional police work with the countering of terrorism. The battle was really on and I began to see the potential within the Catholic community in Newtownhamilton for my murder. I went on the offensive but was careful to be as evenhanded as possible.

We were very close as a unit – Skipper, Max, Jim, George, Tommy, Ritchie and myself, and with our army friends we had many good times – knit together by potential danger and the constant terrorist threat. George and I would travel home in convoy to cover each other – we lived a few miles apart. He had such a dry humour and made me, as a raw recruit, look very foolish at times but he was an excellent policeman with good local knowledge. Skipper was well educated and kept firm control, but allowed us to have fun even at his expense – we loved to do the crossword together. Max had been a policeman a long time and although very helpful and thoughtful at times I was always aware of who the senior man was. Jim loved his drink and unfortunately was controlled by it, but he was so likeable and could have been a fine policeman. Tommy liked to spend his time on cars and odd jobs and it always seemed that his police job was merely subservient to the others. Ritchie loved the girls and his weightlifting. All in all a hotch-potch of minds, strengths, weaknesses and yet one, in an outpost of security and hope for an increasingly beleaguered community.

As time went on and acquaintance after acquaintance became victims of the South Armagh brigade of the I.R.A. I became more frustrated. Bombs in the town centre would go off and we would start all over again. Protestant after Protestant, U.D.R. man after U.D.R. man would fall into pernicious traps and I felt totally helpless. As I walked through the bombed out remains of the shops in the Square, I wondered who it could have been and I longed for the opportunity to catch the culprits. As I walked away I heard an explosion and saw firemen flung through the air – some without limbs, and knowing where I had been a few moments before the hidden bomb exploded, I realised yet again I had cheated death.

The more beleaguered Newtownhamilton became the more united we, as policemen, became in our resolve to protect the people and resist the terrorist — but how frustrating that occupation became. I knew that many of the Roman Catholics in South Armagh were supporting the terrorists and as I checked car boots at the security barrier outside the station, I often thought to myself — who are these people? Were they setting me up? Did they hate me? Did that smile or greeting disguise their contempt? I was sure that I was in a war and

I just couldn't pinpoint the enemy.

Policemen and U.D.R. men and soldiers were dying at the hands of terrorist attacks on an increasing level and the I.R.A. were becoming more savage, more cunning and more equipped. The security forces would have an occasional success and my joy on those rare occasions was usually diluted very soon by another security force or Protestant death. Yet despite the danger around me, the deaths and the destruction, I never feared for my own safety.

# Chapter 3

# Death Face to Face

I was typing out a motoring offence report – George had just taken over a two hour stint on barrier duty from me and I was due to go out again in an hour. Suddenly several sharp, echoing cracks erupted from what appeared to me to be a few yards away – I had heard it before – I knew it was gunfire. Instinctively thinking the station was under attack I ran downstairs, grabbed an S.M.G. (sub machine gun) and ran outside. Soldiers were shouting. People were crouching in doorways but there was no gunfire. I took up my position at the security hut and out of the side of my eye I saw a figure lying on the ground just beside the barrier. I looked – it was George lying on his back. For a few seconds I thought he had fallen whilst taking cover, but as I stooped down and looked at his rolling eyes I realised he was not dying but already dead!

He was a big man, six foot three inches – always immaculate – creased trousers, clean, ironed shirt, clean shaven – he took great pride in his appearance. Yet, as he lay on his back slightly rocking because of his concave but blatantly ineffective flak jacket (bullet-proof vest), death spoke louder than anything I had ever heard. My mind and emotions exploded as I tried to shake George back to life. For the first time in my life I couldn't handle the situation and I sobbed my heart out. I remembered the days that he had angered me with his thoroughness and eye for detail; I remembered the day that we had escaped the terrorist bullets at Cullyhanna; I remembered our races home – he in his Minor 1000, me in my Fiat 128. I remembered his wife and two little girls and emotionally I couldn't cope. The local doctor came and, still clinging to the untenable, I went into the kitchen where his huge frame was stretched out on the table – I had never seen such a pathetic sight – the living genial giant was a cold, blood-smeared corpse.

Emotions were to change over the next few days from intense hatred for the I.R.A. to intense sorrow for a life-shattered widow and two little girls who couldn't understand what was going on. At the funeral I carried the coffin and fought back the tears unsuccessfully, and as I watched the coffin lowered into the grave, I vowed vengeance in memory of my fallen friend.

# Chapter 4
# The S.P.G.

The execution of that vow began in a pathetic way days later, as I grabbed a man I believed to be a terrorist, or at least a supporter, and pushed him through the window of a bombed-out building opposite the station. That was the beginning of the end of my stay in Newtownhamilton, as my apparent hatred forced my sympathetic superiors from Bessbrook to literally arrange a transfer overnight, to the Special Patrol Group based in Armagh. I didn't realise at the time that the authorities had played totally into my hands by placing me in the roughest, toughest, most elite bunch of police officers in the Royal Ulster Constabulary. I bypassed the up to then mandatory interviews for the S.P.G. and I began to serve out a three year period of venting my frustration by terrorising the terrorists or their supporters.

My first night on duty proved that I was at home as our Landrover pulled up beside two young men outside Armagh. The sergeant and the four man crew jumped out and started to question the men. I was enthralled as I watched the sergeant knee one man on the thigh and another crew member flatten the other with a punch in the stomach. This was the outfit for me! I soon realised I was in the midst of a group of about forty men who for the most part were just as venomous and militant as I was – men who had been fighting since 1969 from the streets of Londonderry, to the bandit land of South Armagh, and who by experience knew who the enemy was and had the means and the freedom to do something about it.

The next few years gave me the opportunity to fulfil my vow and play my part in hitting back at the enemy. We were so good at our job that whilst policemen were being killed all over the land we never lost one man despite being right in the forefront of the battle. If there were riots, we were there; if there were reports of armed men in an area we were sent in. We were the first policemen in Ulster to be equipped with rifles and some time later the first to receive S.L.R's (self loading rifles). We needed them, as on several occasions we were called to return fire, or open fire on terrorists. We spearheaded an offensive into South Armagh as we enforced law and order issues on the lawless public from helicopters, equipped with full military equipment. How I loved those road blocks, as we would catch offending motorists who never knew what a road fund licence was. How I loved to walk up the streets of Crossmaglen showing off my police uniform and defiantly gesturing – "We're here to stay!"

Comradeship was supreme as we protected each other and covered for each other, from sergeants to constables. Playing cards together one minute, to drinking or cavorting together the next, to jumping hedges in hot pursuit in South Armagh the next.

Roman Catholics, especially young militant ones, were fair game, and the number of times I satiated my appetite for revenge on their persons are too many to record – hospital records bear witness. My hatred was running amok as I turned to making the life of the one other policeman who was a Catholic in our squad a real misery. He eventually emigrated to Canada.

In the midst of the rampage, tempered with carrying on a semblance of family life with my growing family – now two girls, I began to play rugby for the police, soon displaying the same kamikaze aggression on the rugby field as in my police work. This proved to be somewhat of a release valve for me but I could not hide my hatred for Catholics, by now all branded the same. This would mean me breaking my knuckles twice – once on the rugby field on the jaw of a Catholic police rugby player whom I had targeted earlier, and again on a Catholic member of the rugby club in Armagh, as in a drunken rage I battered him senseless and got suspended.

# Chapter 5

# A Message From the Queen

One morning I received a strange letter through the post. It was marked "Confidential" and had the Royal insignia on it. Absolute shock and unbelief, with a little bewilderment, greeted the unfolding news that I was to receive the Queen's Gallantry Medal from H.M. the Queen at Buckingham Palace. For a moment I could not understand – I thought it was a mistake, but as I studied the letter my mind quickly went back to Newtownhamilton . . .

It was Tuesday court day – the R.M. (Resident Magistrate) was listening to the usual variety of minor motoring cases – I had one man up for "baldy tyres". It was near dinner time and we were just about finished when I heard those familiar gunshot cracks again – it seemed like a machine gun, there were so many. I ran out of the courthouse door and immediately saw a soldier stumble towards the wall surrounding the courthouse. I jumped the wall and pulled the by now fallen man into an entry out of the line of fire. The echo of gunfire reverberated around my mind and head – I didn't know where the shooting was coming from or if it had stopped. I knew the soldier had been shot. I rendered first aid, but it was clear there was no helping him – he soon died. I met Mr. Wilson, the R.M., at the door of the court – blood dripping from my hands, and smeared on my uniform. He stood in silent but marked amazement – my other colleagues, the Sarge, Max, and the Inspector had similarly responded. It was hours later I realised the split second folly and futility of my actions. Several gunmen who had taken over the pub opposite the courthouse awaited the appearance of several casual policemen who would soon come out. A young soldier of the Signal's Regiment who had nipped down to the shop for some onions proved an irresistible and fatal target. His dying meant our living and I realised that SOMEONE HAD DIED IN MY PLACE.

Some twelve months later I was to be on my way, as a result of the Magistrates' recommendation, with my three colleagues to be awarded a Gallantry Medal. A reward for folly – the fine line between bravery and death.

What an experience it was for me as my wife, my mother and I went to London for the first time – a real "puss in boots". We stayed at the Sherlock Holmes Hotel and basked in our fortune – a free trip to London. I can't remember much about the ceremony as I was so awestruck. I do remember the grandiose military men, the top hat and tailed coat brigade. As I was announced to walk into Her Majesty the Queen I was totally amazed. She spoke to me, and for what seemed an eternity I listened, but I still don't recall what she said. She pinned the medal on my chest. I was supposed to salute; I don't know if I did, but as I walked out of the ceremonial room it seemed as if I was royalty itself – I was filled with pride and I so wanted George to be alive to participate in it. My wife told me I was a sight for sore eyes – she was prouder than I. She kept asking me what was said, but I couldn't tell her – I think she thought I was being "contrary". We spent the next hour getting photograph after photograph taken.

We went to London Zoo; we saw the sights; but all too soon we went home to put away the medal and consign it to a fate of relative anonymity and secrecy. I'm not sure that I deserved it; I'm really sure it didn't deserve me! Publicity was forbidden because of the security situation but my prowess and growing stature amongst my S.P.G. colleagues was enhanced and I became very much accepted in the "force within a force"

# Chapter 6

# The Terrorist Lawman

It was during this time that the Protestant backlash grew apace and the murder triangle, which was our area, witnessed some vicious, highly skilled, and well executed attacks on Roman Catholics – gun and bomb attacks on Catholic bars and assassinations in homes. Yet for every Protestant-inspired terrorist attack the I.R.A. would respond with increased violence. For every "Miami Showband" massacre there would be a "Kingsmills" minibus massacre, and funerals abounded. We knew who the terrorists were, and although we would torture them, beat them and intimidate them, we could never convict them. Colleagues were being killed, Protestant neighbours were being killed and nothing seemed to be having any effect.

It was against this background that I decided to cast my lot in with the Protestant terrorist organisation. Firstly to fulfil my vow of vengeance to George but also to hit before being hit – to strike at the strikers – to terrorise the terrorists. Several of my S.P.G. friends felt the same way and so began a series of terrorist ventures aimed at terrorists that was to go on for many months. During this time gun and bomb attacks took place; terrorists were terrorised and information valuable to terrorist-seekers was given. We used our influence, our knowledge and our position to make war on the terrorists, and for the first time we felt we were making an impression. I thrived on every moment of action, living four lives at once – the husband of my wife and father of my children; the policeman; the rugby player and the terrorist – a life of sheer undiluted deception.

I entered the Sergeant's exam, and in between 12 hour shifts of duty with the army in South Armagh I studied. I applied myself well and passed quite easily but my youth ensured that promotion did not come too quickly.

In the Police I continued to rebel against authority and was always gesturing my rebellion in some way – whether it was throwing buckets of water on unsuspecting police officers from the roof of the station, to lighting pieces of newspapers placed under the rear collar of the driver or Sergeant in the front – it was always fun but danger always lurked close by. I never was much of a driver but I certainly gave my colleagues the most memorable 12th July they ever had. I drove the long wheel-based Landrover, armour plated, top heavy and extremely hard to handle. Just my luck to be following one of the best drivers in the unit. In attempting to keep pace down a steep decline I just lost control – the Landrover hit the high-sided kerb, veered all over the road and somehow or other came to a halt with everyone in the Rover wondering how. We called our Sarge "Yellow Charlie", but his reputation of being easily frightened wasn't helped by his leaping over the wall on our stopping. Everyone thought it hilarious as he took refuge behind the tree cum toilet. I was just embarassed. Foolishly I continued to drive, but the constant slagging and abuse from the "sympathetic" crew, coupled with my desire to give as good as I got, meant me losing my concentration and thus when the Landrover in front stopped, I kept going! The Landrover adopted a new shape and my misery was complete. I wasn't prosecuted but then again no-one ever remembered an S.P.G. man who had been. My driving escapades continued, as did my accidents, but as I reflected on that speedy uncontrolled dice with death on the road to Kilkeel, I realised that with others I COULD HAVE BEEN KILLED.

My promotion eventually came and with it my transfer to Lurgan. I wished I hadn't passed. I hated the thought of leaving the S.P.G. and my friends – yet I wanted to be a Sergeant. My ambition was stronger and after the customary stag night of celebration I left to become a Sergeant in Lurgan. I also left behind my personal activity in the unofficial war against the I.R.A.

My years in Lurgan were a nightmare as I battled against the authorities, the I.R.A. and myself. Policemen continued to die from Inspector to Reserve Officers, men and women. I led from the front and alienated some less committed men and my Senior Officers. With my Sergeant friend I continued my vendetta against Roman Catholics and used every chance, to book, batter or break them. This was an eventful time in my police career. I was now consumed by my rugby activities, alcohol, and parties on or off duty. James and I would go "mickey hunting" after these parties and eventually we went too far. My car number was taken by a victim of an aggressive assault and three of us were suspended whilst investigations took place. I wasn't charged but my friends were, only to be acquitted to our celebratory delight, and customary two finger salute to the authorities. I was disciplined and was the first officer to be suspended whilst already suspended for further extra police activity. I received a warning and a transfer. I didn't regret the move to Portadown, but as I reflected on the events of Lurgan I was sure that sooner or later the taming had to come. Whilst in Lurgan I had treated with contempt the dangers of working in a town ravaged by terrorists. One night James and I walked into a Chinese Restaurant in response to a "bomb call", having spent most of our tour of duty boozing. We opened the carrier bag, looked at each other, and James said "It's a Chinese bomb!" We beat a hasty retreat as the sense of self-preservation and duty took over – five minutes later we had cleared the close proximity, only to hear our Chinese bomb go off and watch the building through the smoke and dust collapse into a heap of rubble. How those Chinese bemoaned their "victimisation". We thought it quite funny in a way and wondered who did it – were they Protestant Chinese or Catholic Chinese? As I thought about the bomb in the bag I realised that the victims of its power could have included me.

On another occasion I was leading a patrol of Landrovers, as we did a roadcheck late at night on the outskirts of Lurgan – the Republican end. Nothing was untoward about the roadcheck – pretty routine – until several sharp gunshot cracks resounded. Along with the driver of the Landrover I flung myself towards the ground, cocking my sub machine gun as I nestled against the hedge. I didn't know where the shots had come from but the terrorists weren't to know that. So I opened up with my machine gun firing several single shots into the air. A voice from the midst of the hedge shouted, "Well done, skipper – fire away!" I stopped firing – no more shots came – the road stop was ended and we returned to base. The faceless enemy had once again made an attempt to kill – unsuccessfully, but I never thought that I was a key target, not because of who I was, but because of what I wore!

Family life was very much curtailed at this time. We never went on holiday as a family and between rugby and police duty I only used my home as a garage – fill up during the day and parking at night.

With my growing appetite for I.R.A. hunting came my closer association with members of terrorist Protestant organisations. Socialising and working together I felt that our objectives were fulfilling my ambition to the utmost. This association and co-operation took many forms and was always mutually beneficial.

# Chapter 7

# Don't Rock the Boat

I will never forget the day that several of us set off in a little boat from Kilkeel to sail to the Isle of Man. If the Special Branch had stopped that boat, what a selection of hardened, professional Protestant terrorists they would have found, with a police Sergeant stuck in the midst! We had a good day at the T.T. but coming home I realised the folly of our venture. A storm blew up and I realised the boat we six men were in, wasn't big enough to hold two! — my little girls played with bigger boats in the bath! The little outboard motor was making no headway against the pounding, raging waves – if anything, it seemed we were going backwards. Debate raged whether to turn back or forge ahead! Whether to laugh or cry, whether to curse or pray. Me? I wanted to turn back. I cried and I prayed on my knees as never before – "Lord if you get me home, I'll be a changed man!!"

We got home and I was a changed man – for two days, and then forgot my deliverance and reckoned it was just a "storm in a teacup". Today, I realise, having heard of so many lost at sea who were much better prepared than we, I really should and COULD HAVE BEEN DROWNED.

On another occasion, a friend was caught doing an armed robbery and ended up in a cell at Lurgan police station. I took the opportunity to visit him. That night he escaped through a window in his cell.

I was totally committed to the anti-I.R.A. cause and anyone associated with them was fair game from the legitimate or illegitimate line of approach for me. I rejoiced when suspected I.R.A. men were brought into Lurgan station and were put through the rack of mental and physical torture. I would listen through the lift as down in the interview room suspects were made to do exercises, beaten up, screamed at etc. – sometimes to great effect and at other times to no avail. In a way I had a grudging respect for those who said nothing despite all the pressure. When they would walk free with no charges I was confirmed in my belief that alternative means were the only means to bring these men's reign of terror to an end. I also knew I was not alone in this view – my terrorist friends would tell me of times when they had been arrested for activities and questioned by C.I.D. or Special Branch. Whilst in custody they were given the names and addresses of I.R.A. hitmen and told that investigations into such "assassinations" as might occur would be far from exhaustive. The truth of the matter was that when such investigations did occur they didn't need to be exhaustive, as most Protestants in the main readily confessed to their part in illegal activities. I hated the C.I.D. when they nailed Protestant extremists for murdering Republicans – I was becoming more and more of an entrenched, sectarian excuse for a police sergeant.

One of the results of my wayward and rebellious activities was a disciplinary hearing at Police H.Q. I was charged with several misdemeanours, but having pleaded guilty to two, I got the others dropped. My past record and my superiors' references enabled me to escape with a reprimand and to resume duty, but with a transfer to nearby Portadown. It was around this time that I felt a need to talk religion – I can't explain why. I had been going to the Presbyterian Church irregularly, mainly due to the need of baptisms – my family was growing – three girls, Michelle, Adelle and Danielle. I never heard a word the minister said, yet it was at this time I realised that the boozing, fighting, disciplinary action etc. was weighing me down. I asked my Minister Rev. Anderson to come and see me. He talked through my problems and pointed me to my responsibilities. I must have looked a sight – two little girls, a baby girl, a broken hand, (I had broken it on a Catholic's head fighting in the rugby club ), suspended from the Police and still only 24 years of age. He was faithful, although I don't remember what was said, and left me a booklet which I never read. A few weeks passed and I was back at work, the plaster off and things looking up again – I never thought another thing about the Rev. Anderson's talk.

The opportunity came to go to America with the Rugby Club and I threw my lot into fundraising in the hope that I would be chosen. Despite a knee injury I was chosen and in 1978 with twenty others plus, we flew to Boston and began a tour which would take us to Concorde, New Hampshire and on to New York. From the outset it was one big drinking, drug-taking, women-chasing adventure – thrills having to be sponsored by beer, cocaine and nightclubs. I cannot deny how much I enjoyed those eighteen days – I loved the country, the people and the lifestyle and when we left three of our merry band behind as illegal immigrants, I envied them so much. I never did play a rugby match but I certainly played the field of wild oat sowing and brought home with me memories bad and good. Even in America I could not escape my history and sectarian emotions as we spent an evening in an "Irish Bar", and whilst the regulars waited on our rendering of the "Soldiers Song" we sang "The Sash" and were hurriedly ejected from great impending danger. I couldn't escape my heritage and didn't intend to dilute it either.

# Chapter 8

# Kidnapped!

I wasn't home from America many months
when one Saturday night, very late, I got a
phone call – it was Willy. The gist of the
message was very simple – Billy Turbitt, a
policeman from Bessbrook, and Hugh
McConnell, a reserve policeman from
Bessbrook, had been ambushed by the I.R.A. at
Forkhill, South Armagh. Hugh was dead! Billy
had been kidnapped and was being held by the
I.R.A. Action was needed to recover Billy and
was I prepared to be a party to a plan to win
his freedom? I was the man! Of course, without
hesitation I would do whatever was necessary.

I got changed and told Roberta that I was
going on a job – she understood. I was filled
with two emotions – great sadness at Hughie's
death – (he was a personal friend, having
served, played football and gone to England
together, and now he was gone). I was excited
at the possibility of doing something to win
back another friend and colleague whom I had
served with for years and known so well. Had
I realised then that Billy had not survived the
ambush and died immediately, with his body

being taken for propaganda purposes, I would not be writing this, but I took no time to find out the facts – I was ready for action.

That action took me via Lurgan and Willy's home to pick up the weapons and on to Ahoghill, Co. Antrim, where en route I learnt of the plan – to kidnap a Roman Catholic priest and exchange him for Billy – simple and surely effective! Such was my pathetic appreciation of the situation that it saw me drive to a safe area to kidnap an ex R.A.F. Chaplain and use him as an exchange with a group of hardened, merciless, cold-blooded killers. I threw myself wholeheartedly into it without thinking about how such an exchange might take place if successful, who was going to look after the victim, who was going to mediate, etc. etc. I just wanted Billy back with his family in Richill and out of the hands of the men whom I could envisage torturing and demeaning him.

The two of us arrived at the home of Father Murphy and parked the car down the drive. I pulled on my balaclava and stood around the corner, a Browning pistol in my hand, whilst Willy acted the part of a needy parishioner and called Father Murphy from his bed – it was early morning on Sunday. He duly came to the door and I got the call to come and get our man. We called each other strange names but I kept forgetting what Willy's should be as he got Mick, Sean, and any other such like name I could think of. We landed our victim into the hallway and I got my first sight of this bartering agent. What a pathetic sight it was, an old, thin, balding, bespectacled man in a dressing gown covering his striped pyjamas. His calls to be left alone were roughly denied and very quickly he was made aware that it was for real and he was being kidnapped. He then pleaded for two things – his cigarettes and holy water – a very strange combination, but he got both and we led this poor frightened slippered man blindfolded down the lane and into the seat of the car. I kept the gun to his head as Billy drove and I still didn't know exactly where we were going. We carried on small chat as the priest vainly tried to ascertain what was happening. He was left under no illusion that his life was in danger and the gun pointed at his head was no idle threat. As I fingered the trigger I was under no illusion either – if he struggled or tried to escape I would have to shoot him!

We took long cuts to our safe house – Willy's parent's home – a few miles away and in an outhouse we tied our prisoner up. Willy had done most of the talking, assuring the priest of our best intentions and our design. After the initial shock and rough treatment a relationship developed and as Willy discussed the issue, albeit briefly, I began to feel sorry for this old man who seemed to be the lousiest example of Republican extremism that I could envisage. I slowly but surely grew to realise we were going nowhere but I wasn't going to admit it. We gave our prisoner tea and biscuits and tried to make him comfortable – I no longer had the heart to hurt or scare him and I came to the conclusion that I had done my part and was heading home. Arrangements were made for the securing of our victim and now all that remained was publicity! We stopped at a phone box. I went to it and rang the local radio station Downtown. With a firm and monotone voice I asked for the news branch and deliberately, quietly told them that I was speaking on behalf of the Ulster Freedom Fighters (I wanted it to be as fearsome as possible) and that Father Murphy was in our custody and would be released when Billy Turbitt was released, otherwise he would be killed. Before my respondent could ask any questions I hung up. Now we could only wait.

I arrived home and went to church. I spent the day perfectly normally – visiting my grandmother and basking in all the publicity that was abounding over the kidnapping of Father Murphy. I inwardly giggled as my loved ones debated the pros and cons of the action – "I hope they shoot him" – "What's the point, they won't release the policeman" – "Why didn't they go for Father F . . . ?" "About time somebody did something." "What do you think, Gary?"

"Time would tell", I said, but I was beginning to get a little concerned as evening came. I was shattered when Rev. Ian Paisley came on the news to condemn the act and demand the release of the priest. I realised that our actions had been wrongly directed and I rang Willy to say that I felt the priest should be released – such a decision had already been made and the priest was dumped on the roadside late Sunday night, physically unharmed – but mentally?

I really thought little more about it, apart from feeling that at least we had tried something and whilst others were talking we were doing.

A couple of weeks later Billy's body was found and I attended his funeral in Richill. How futile my lost night of sleep and my vain action seemed as I followed that coffin and reflected what a loser I really was when it came to carrying out my promise after George's death – yet I was determined to carry on the war.

After this I settled down in some ways, for although still playing rugby and still serving as a police sergeant, my terrorist activities and connections simmered. I still took advantage of lax police security to equip my friends but I was no longer as active as I had been. In many ways I wanted to adopt a lower profile. Roberta was pregnant for the fourth time. My police work was interesting and I was thinking of taking the Inspector's exam.

# Chapter 9

# Arrested

Then December 11th 1978! – I had been on nights and had got up about 5 p.m. It was Adelle's birthday and we had my wife's sister and family in for the birthday party. There was a knock on the door and I found three men standing at the door. One introduced himself as an Inspector and produced his I.D. – he quietly explained the nature of his visit. He wanted to search my home under the Emergency Provisions Act and to arrest me under Section 10. To this day I can't explain my response, because there wasn't any. I led the detectives through my home. They took an air gun that I had received when in Newtownhamilton and for some strange reason looked through my clothing cupboards. I explained to Roberta that I was being arrested and would be back soon as I had done nothing – she assuredly accepted that and I left my family to carry on the birthday party, somehow believing I might be back before it ended. As I travelled to Castlereagh holding centre not a word was spoken and my mind raced in an effort to catch up with what was happening. Several acts of illegality went through my mind but I could not understand what my fellow officers were acting upon.

I had been to Castlereagh on numerous occasions doing prison escorts, but I had never been in the holding centre – it just wasn't dawning on me what I was in for. I was confident that I would quickly handle the situation and put my police experience to use in avoiding any bother. I was soon to be made aware of the gravity of the situation.

Across the table sat a Chief Inspector and he quickly put it to me that I had been involved in the kidnapping of Father Murphy. I denied it flatly and forcefully, but my mind was blasted by the charge and my heart was betraying inwardly what I was endeavouring to present outwardly – a resolute and innocent denial. Pathetically I called for my Police Federation representative, only to be told in no uncertain terms that the nature of the offence was beyond his defending. The facts and fancies of the kidnapping were presented and I was both discouraged and encouraged – discouraged at the knowledge that they knew I was involved, but encouraged by the absence of facts showing that they had only part of the story. Before long I was squirming in my denials, but deny it I did.

That night in a cell on a hard bed I sweated and shivered, not realising the deliberate turning up and down of the heat was to keep me awake and unsettled, but I slept and in a weird way looked forward to the next round of interrogation. It was early morning when this took place but nothing had changed except the interviewers who were to be my constant companions for the next six days. Assertions! Denials! Small talk! Quiet conversation! Noisy exchanges!

On the third day things were to change as I was confronted with the facts that hadn't been presented before, down to the colour of the jumper I wore. Willy had betrayed me! He had told everything and I was caught in a trap. Yet I denied my involvement but not with the same vehemence – I was breaking. The police's breakthrough came when they walked in with the jumper I had worn and told me it was going to forensic science. My police training started to work against me as I was given long periods just to think in my cell. I knew forensic evidence could link my jumper with perhaps Father Murphy's dressing gown – fibres exchanged. I knew that Willy's father and mother were in custody and that they may give evidence against me. I was in desperation, as for the first time I effectively realised my plight.

Things were to get worse. My friends and police comrades involved with me in various other acts of terrorism were also in custody and soon I was being questioned about other incidents, with too many certain facts to give me any assurance other than that someone who was involved was telling everything. I cursed Willy and longed for the opportunity to meet him long enough to strangle him – my hatred for him matched that of any I had for the I.R.A. Soon civilians who had provided bases and arms were in custody and the whole network was exposed. Arms and ammunition were found all over the country including stolen police weapons. It was all up. Yet for some time I kept denying my involvement. I knew silence was the best means of defense for the terrorist, but silent I couldn't keep. No, I wouldn't admit, but I couldn't deny with the same authority. On the fourth morning a Chief Inspector came in to see me and summarized my predicament. Assurances of help with threats of arrest of my pregnant wife, who had known some of my involvement, brought me suddenly and unexpectedly to surrender and I made a statement admitting my involvement with the kidnapping – the nail in my coffin!

If I thought that that was it, I was in for a rude awakening. The pressure was on as never before as questioning on incident after incident took place. I'm sure the detectives thought that the floodgates would open but quite the opposite. I was determined to make no further concession and for two further days I enjoyed the battle of wits and relished stupidly my victory in saying or admitting nothing more. It evolved over the next few days that my police friends Barry, Ivan and Jack had also surrendered as my interrogators brought me news of their admitting different offences at intervals. The greatest surprise to me was Jack. Although I had been in illegitimate action with him and he was probably my closest friend I never knew he had been involved in the murder for which he was charged and later convicted. Awfully I drew solace from the fact that my plight was far less than his, and my interpretation of my actions for which I was being charged left me with an ignorant sense of pride. Yet I was devastated. I would lie in my eight by six cell on my bed and ask God to open the doors and let me out. If I was ill I sent for the doctor. Now I was in trouble I would send for the God who rescued me from the angry waves and protected me from the bomb and bullet – it was not to be.

I was charged with kidnapping and with my friends remanded to appear at a Special Court. I slept in the same cell as Jack that night and saw just how well off I was. He was absolutely devastated, and as we rehearsed our predicament I couldn't help but feel sorry for him – his involvement was circumferential but his fate was sealed.

We were to appear at the Special Court the next morning. My wife and brother came down and Roberta showed great fortitude as my brother praised my loyalist dedication in action. The next 24 hours saw me face a court with its hungry news media and enter into Crumlin

Road prison for what was to be an unforgettable fifteen months.

I stood arraigned in an antiquated oak enclosure with my friend on that morning in the Magistrates Court. The courtroom was packed – reporters, news media, policemen, lawyers, and barely noticeable in the crowd, members of my family. The Magistrate took his place and I listened as the charge of kidnapping Father Hugh Murphy, possession of firearms etc., were read out. As instructed I boldly declared "Not Guilty" to all the charges and sat down as the Police presented to the Magistrate a copy of my statement. In no time the Magistrate directed that there was a case to answer and that I should be remanded in custody to appear at a further hearing. I nodded my head at my wife and brother as I left the courtroom feeling no emotion. Despite the fact that such scenes were commonplace to me from the other side, I felt a sense of bewilderment and confusion.

# Chapter 10

# H.M. Prison

I was taken with my friend Jack, who was charged with murder, to Crumlin Road prison in a police van. I could never forget the walk from that van in the custody of two policemen through the old prison corridors to the reception area. The prison officers seemed to be just as embarrassed as me and seemed to want to cheer me up. One came up to me as I stood waiting to undress for weighing and the doctor's examination and said "You only done what the rest of us hadn't the guts to do". It didn't cheer me up as the dark, archaic cold walls began to depress me. I wasn't to realise until I talked to my friends later that I was spared many degrading formalities in reception. I was not asked to strip, nor to take a shower, as they were.

I was conducted by prison officers to cells reserved for incoming prisoners. Mine was warm but very poorly decorated and if its aim was to further depress it certainly worked. I was given books but couldn't read, and food but couldn't eat – plastic eating utensils on a stainless steel tray with various settings, seemed so unreal.

I wanted to be with Jack but he was obviously so distressed that no one was allowed near him. The Presbyterian Minister, Mr. Vance, came but I never heard a word he said. My mind was taking in the full import of what was happening and bewilderment was being replaced by shock.

The night lasted an eternity on a four inch mattress on springs that turned the bed into the shape of a hammock. I tossed and turned as I devised ways to "beat the rap" – as I murdered in my mind the "traitor", as I tried to remove the battery from my mind to stop it ticking over to no avail. I was in an antiquated prison lying in a prison bed eating prison grub and surrounded by prison guards. I was on the receiving end and I didn't like it.

Different officers came in. Some said little, others sympathised, others would have me believe I was a hero, others were cold and formal, but their uniforms said more that their words – I was a prisoner.

The next day I went before the Assistant Governor and he went through the ritual of telling me what was expected from me. He was dispassionate and most matter of fact. I was to be put into the protection wing "A" Wing – A3 and that was to be my home for the next fifteen months.

As I was led into the Wing I got a glimpse of prison life: prisoners in brown uniforms mopping the floors, others in civvies being led by prison officers. Keys would turn in an endless succession of iron barred gates and I was so conscious that every eye was on me. I had made the news – "Police Sergeant charged with kidnapping priest" and it was as if a rare specimen was being paraded for the spectators – a caged animal.

I was put into an empty cell. Two beds in a 12' x 6' cell and as I sat down on one, my sense of total dejection was complete. I looked around. The high arched stone roof, the multi-miniature paned window with bars to the outside and with three panes broken, the "po's" under the bed and the navy blue mattress, all combined to oppress my mind and cause me to groan from within. I knew Jack was close by but I couldn't communicate with him. I felt so alone and helpless.

Well meaning officers and prisoners looked through the peep hole and examined the "exhibit", but I went to sleep, pondering the unknown. I was rudely awakened by the clank of the door lock being opened and a prison officer in the doorway. "Slop Out!" he shouted. I didn't know what he meant but an orderly soon explained that I should empty my pot and go to the waste disposal room. That ritual was to be the first of the most humiliating and soul-destroying exercises ever forced upon any human being, yet probably good medicine for the pride-hardened hearts of the prison's inmates. I hated it. In the following fifteen months I was to use it only in a dire emergency and with unfading embarrassment.

It was some two days of 8 a.m. rising, slopping out, breakfast, exercise for half an hour, dinner, slop out, tea, slop out and lights out, before I was moved from my cell to another, but it came just in time. The previous night I was overcome by a tremendous sense of sorrow for my grandmother. I fought a losing battle against the tears as I considered that dear old lady now in her late seventies who raised me, loved me and esteemed me, yet I wondered if I ever would see her alive. I had never known my heart feel so heavy as self-pity mingled with great concern and love for my dear grandmother. My wife didn't feature, I suppose because her great strength contrasted so greatly with my grandmother's weakness and vulnerability. I don't think I could have taken the loneliness much more.

# Chapter 11

# Freedom

Sure enough I was moved and it was into the cell of another ex-policeman who had been charged with firearms offences with his colleagues, having targeted I.R.A. men's homes, as he supposed! Without much publicity he and his colleagues were charged and had been in prison for some months awaiting trial. His colleagues had moved out to allow me to move in. Robert soon made me feel at ease and his genuine interest and common understanding did so much to comfort me. Although we talked about the incidents we were involved in, I was strangely aware of our surroundings – everything was neat in this cell, the same size, decor, shape, etc., as mine. It was really homely, with photographs on the walls, books on shelves and bed clothes nicely folded. He shared biscuits, fruit and sweets with me and just befriended me.

As the day went on into the evening and he explained to me the prison system, the good officers and the bad, I felt much less depressed and it seemed a strangely natural progression when he moved on to speak about God and how God had helped him through his time of trial. I was really interested as he told how he had slipped from a life of church- going and Christian commitment, into the anti-I.R.A. cause and how trouble had brought him back to God and that was the way he intended it to remain. He talked through with me the story of God's love in his life and what this man Jesus meant to him. I felt such sincerity from him and knew that every word he was saying was true – here I was believing the "Gospel" from a prisoner in a prison cell, when years and months before I had derided, persecuted, and berated Christians in the police force.

I was very quickly learning the lesson that a mind can change when circumstances dictate they should. The crutches of booze, rugby, mates, family, had all been removed and I knew I was floundering. Robert's advice to give my life in my hour of need to a God I couldn't see, never recognise and barely knew about, seemed so legitimate that my emotion and my mind wanted to know more. For hours we talked about the Bible, Christianity, Christ, God, and sin, and everything he said which once seemed outlandish and incredible, sounded not only plausible but very, very relevant – it was God and me!

I can't remember the exact words Robert spoke as I entered into sleep but I will always remember what I did as I closed my eyes – I asked God to forgive my past and to give me a new start. He knew my need and I desperately wanted to change. I told God that the life that had promised me pleasure had now brought me pain; the life that had promised me honour had brought me disgrace; the life that had promised me happiness had brought me and those dear to me great misery. I wanted Him to come into my life and plot a new course. I was conscious as I slept the night hours away that I was in deep communion with God and sleep seemed so sweet, and peaceful.

When I awoke I startled myself with Godward thoughts and told Robert what I had done. He rejoiced and we prayed to God together. How naturally he prayed to God, not as I had known in my church at home. He just talked to God and spoke in tones and with such depth of meaning that I knew his relationship to God was no flash in the pan. I prayed out loud, encouraged by Robert's "Amen" and "Praise the Lord" and there began some of the noisiest most blessed prayer meetings that Crumlin Road had ever experienced. I needed no encouragement to read the Bible and talk "Christian Turkey" – I had an insatiable appetite. It soon became clear that Robert had been playing the part of a missionary in A3 and several prisoners including his colleagues had become Christians. They had weekly meetings in a hall at the end of the corridor and I was soon to be invited. The news of my salvation quickly spread and brought various reactions.

"Prison religion again", from one officer, "Glory to God, welcome to the family", from another. "Can't do your wack, Sergeant Armstrong", from the IRA Provo commander on A1. Yet no-one could shake me from the blessed assurance that I was changing and knew it – I didn't want to curse and it hurt me when I did. What a change from my vocabulary of four letter words punctuating every sentence! I didn't want to read the seedy books but loved Christian books such as "The Cross and the Switchblade" and "The Hiding Place". I read and read. I prayed and prayed and forgot somehow or another the awful predicament I was in.

I wanted to tell everyone and that meant first my wife and family. On their first visit, without any tact or preparation, I blurted it out – "I've been born again and I'm so very happy". *They must have thought I had blown a fuse!*

Very soon I was joined by my two comrades – Barry, charged with attempted murder, bombing etc. and Ivan likewise. Having become an old timer of three days duration and having followed the news of their being charged and remanded, I was only too ready to offer my comfort and of course my good news. Others were charged at the same time from the Force, but they never joined us on A Wing. They were quickly released on bail. Ivan and Barry were in together and were good support for each other but in the early strange stages they too went through that period of bewilderment and shock.

Meanwhile Jack went from bad to worse and it soon became clear that he was desperately sick, suffering from the shock of his predicament and his total inability to come to terms with the import of it, both present and future. It came as no surprise to hear that he had been taken to the prison hospital where he was to spend the majority of the next fifteen months. Efforts to rehabilitate him and slip him into our mainstream were abysmal failures as he slipped from initial signs of recovery into deep depression and a display of suicidal tendencies. My plea for him to turn to Christ and find in Him a resting place was partially recognised but Jack was in too deep a depression and was looking too much inward to be able to lift his eyes. I read the rhyme "Two men looked from prison bars, one saw mud, the other stars". Jack was mud spotting and I was star gazing. We saw each other occasionally at remand court, or services and short periods he could cope with. In fact he was always optimistic about his chances, but drugs and artificial supports hid from him the real situation. I was thriving on the finest of the wheat, rejoicing in my Saviour, witnessing, praying, reading. He was on hunger strike and pathetically grabbing at straws. I was leaning on Christ. He was leaning on a fast melting iceberg. He was later to put his trust in Christ and although never shining as a city on a hill he nonetheless went forward.

# Chapter 12

# Partners Again

It was the last Sunday in December when two Christian policemen called on my wife at home. They were sent by God in answer to many prayers, not least mine, and their witness to her of her need to join me in the ranks of the "redeemed" needed no forceful arguments – she was ripe for the plucking. Her circumstances and the change she readily admitted seeing in me convinced her that Christ was right for her. She responded that Sunday evening and committed her life and future to her husband's Saviour and found him to be her Saviour too. What a joy it was to learn on her next visit and we rejoiced with no little emotion as we were truly joined together as never before possible. This really set the ball rolling as next my mother came to profess salvation – what a miracle that was! A sick, alcohol-hardened, cigarette smoking mother who had no time for God, was mightily transformed and it became soon apparent the reality and depth of her conversion. She was followed by Roberta's sister who professed salvation and soon we were hearing of others. One domino had fallen and we gave God the glory for the knock-on effect.

I soon received a visit from a Christian policeman as well. He arrived to visit me and told me that he had learnt of my conversion and shared his faith with me. The whole point of the visit became clear when I was asked if I did not now feel I should make a clean breast of all my past wrongdoings – confess all! I resented the use of my new found faith as a lever to open the door to my vicious past and I closed the door firmly by saying, *"The blood of Jesus cleanseth me from all sin"*. I told them that no-one would gain by any further disclosures and God was not holding me to ransom for my past. I would forget those things that were behind and press towards the mark – the familiar and age-old debate about accountability to God versus accountability to man! Repentance versus retribution etc. raged for a few minutes before the meeting was called to a halt and I excused myself. I was to think on the arguments for some days, asking God to overcome fear or favour to reveal His will for me and His directions as to my past. I realised through His Word that no money, no words and no acts could put right what I had done wrong. The past was buried in the sea of His forgetfulness and He had placed a "No Fishing" sign on its surface. My stand was to be vindicated some fifteen months later.

My range of emotions changed much over the next few weeks. Joy in times of prayer with

Robert; peace in times of reading; love in times with my wife and family; comfort in times with my friends; hope in times with my advisors through to sadness at my being rejected by my friends who deemed me to be a religious fanatic. There was also fear at hearing my name shouted from the I.R.A. cells below me. "Sergeant Armstrong, we know where you live. We'll get you". (I didn't know how real those threats were to prove.) Disappointment as my application for bail was turned down (the police opposed it on the grounds that I had been involved in other crimes and further charges were likely); and uncertainty as to what would ultimately happen.

We formed a little group. Six policemen in the midst of sexual perverts, informers, runaways from the organisations, "hoods" (ordinary criminals who were not welcome amongst the organisations such as U.V.F., I.R.A., U.D.A. etc.) – never exposed to attack – always under the watchful eye of the prison officers. The drawback was that we spent 23 hours out of 24 hours in our cell, (apart from visits, slopping out, collecting meals etc.). We showered separately, we had our own religious meetings separately, we were kept on our own in the Sunday Services. Although we recognised the need for this protection it only served to increase the tension and isolation felt.

Days turned into weeks and weeks into months. Christmas rolled on to Easter and soon the bright days came, prolonging the time. My first Christmas was indeed a time never to be forgotten. Most of the prison officers were sympathetic and a few downright spoiled us, opening our cells to allow us to visit each other, sitting in and chatting with us, giving us reading materials etc. I ate so much on Christmas Day as officers brought huge amounts of extra grub that I had to make myself sick to relieve myself, much to the amusement of my cell mate. We learnt to be innovative, keeping meats cool by placing them outside between the glass panes and bars, boiling water on the piping hot pipes running through the cell and making tea or coffee etc. etc.

We always knew when there would be searches and could ensure that nothing was able to cause offence.

We had visits three times a week and my wife would never fail to come and see me, whatever the weather. What lovely times those were as Christian love abounded. I loved writing letters but was allowed only three per week which I felt I should use as tools of evangelism to friends, so I wrote on small pieces of paper and folded them into such tiny lumps, hiding them inside the waistband of my trousers. Apart from once when I was stripsearched, no officer really bothered, and I was never caught. I would then smuggle it to my beloved. She still has them! Letters were a delight to me. Sending and receiving, many doors were opened, new friends made and many lessons learnt. I wrote to all sorts. From Oral Roberts to Henri's Revivals, I was learning to sift the wheat from the chaff. Mistakes abounded but so did the blessings! I would read my Bible and come up with questions which I would write down. I would then send them to my friend Norman who spent the next month with elders, ministers and the whosoever, finding the answers to the simpleton's inquisitive and curious mind. Most answers were acceptable, some were not, but I was content to allow God to keep hold on the secret things. I just wanted to be able to practice what I did know.

I was hungry for God and soon started to take Bible studies, sharing my limited understanding. I would not accept everything at face value, nor was I going to fit into a nicely made religiously labelled suit. I wanted to know about baptism; I wanted to know about the gifts of the Holy Spirit; I wanted to know about the End Times; I wanted to know about the Lord's Supper; but I had no teacher, well, no pastor that is. Yet I had the Holy Spirit and I gave myself totally to Him to lead me into truth. When I came to conclusions such as every believer should be baptised by full immersion in water, my Baptist friends were delighted; when I came to the conclusion that a post-conversion experience of God's anointing power to equip for service and the edification of God's Church, was available, whatever it might be termed, my

Pentecostal friends were delighted; when I came to the conclusion that the Lord's Table was the central theme of Sunday Worship Service and should be celebrated simply and joyfully each Sunday, my Brethren friends were delighted; but somehow I found it hard to understand why each group could not tolerate me believing all of these experiences – I soon learnt the meaning of denominalisation and I grieve over it as much today as I grieved then.

Some months after I moved in with Robert, familiarity bred contempt and 23 hours together, seven days a week, took its toll. Christian brotherhood made way for monastic brotherhood as we silently ignored each other. It was time for a change, and in came Barry, my friend and comrade. He had by this time made a commitment to Christ also, but felt I was going overboard and there was no need for all the prayer and Bible reading etc. Barry was a real countryman, but years of experience and a very high intelligence rating made him a most remarkable cell mate. For many months we enjoyed each other's company and shared each other's secrets. A real conversationalist, he made my time go by so quickly in those first months with his stories, experiences and jokes. It was whilst we were together that we went through a period when prison officers were being murdered by the I.R.A. The officers took action by stopping visits, food parcels, letters, and exercise. For 24 hours a day, seven days a week, we never left the cell – slopping out into a bucket, washing in a dish. It was really a very hard time for us, but we prevailed and came through putting it down to experience and thanking God for the opportunity to learn from it.

Confrontations with the official clergy were frequent, although always amicable. Though registered Presbyterian, I insisted on going to the free Presbyterian services rather than the mixed services – I was learning quickly about separation, and I could see that regular services were mere forms, whereas the free services were power-packed and joy-filled with real deep meaningful fellowship abounding. I'll always be thankful to Mr. McIlveen for his marvellous leadership and great Christian counsel to me in those days. Such could not be found elsewhere and although I respected the other clergymen as people, I could not hold to their positions, and as was my unfortunate wont, told them so! Grace overcame and we agreed to disagree but as Barry would testify, I did love a debate and I did hate to lose it!

# Chapter 13

# A Child is Born

During those fifteen months I experienced real highs and real lows in the humdrum, the hubbub and the confusion of the prison system. First the lows – I lost a tooth when the prison dentist felt that the tooth removal rate was too low and turned my toothache into a tooth gap! The day I was served my papers outlining the prosecution case I was devastated – I just could not believe what I was reading and felt I would probably be hanged! The day the dear friend who led me to the Lord received four years when everyone thought he would go free. And the highs – the night when the prison officer fulfilled my prophecy made one hour earlier to Barry and told me that God had given my wife and I our greatly longed-after son – Aaron James Moses Armstrong – the day my wife told me that my two eldest girls, Michelle and Adelle, had given their lives to the Lord at a children's midweek meeting – the day I applied for and got bail in the High Court.

That was the day I'll never forget. Going through more formality – holding little hope and much prayer. I was completely taken aback when the judge, against the advice of the Police, said he could see no reason why I should not be allowed out on bail and ordered my bail release. I could have shouted "Hallelujah" and my feet never touched the ground as I went back to my cell to gather my belongings and arrange my collection. Roberta hadn't even bothered to come down for the application. My joy was tinged with sadness at the thoughts of leaving my friends behind, for although Barry and I some months before had developed a cold war of our own and split into single cells, we were by now very good friends.

My, what a different world – earth around is sweeter green, skies above are softer blue, something lives in every hue, Christless eyes have never seen. No greater object lesson could my Heavenly Father have taught me by my thirteen months in prison. It was as if everything was revolutionarily changed. I was taken aback at the feeling of freedom and I am sure my conversation to Roberta and my friend Norman was, to say the least, strange. What a day of reunion that was as my family all got together – for first thing we did was to kneel and thank God for my release. Three weeks of bliss with my wife and family saw me get up each morning at 6 a.m. to walk in the nearby woods, and opened my eyes for the first time to the beauty and magnificence of God's created order. That first morning of freedom I just stood and looked at the green grass and trees, the running river and the lovely flowers. I heard for the first time effectively the singing of the birds – I felt the gentle brush of the breeze – What a wonderful world!

On that first Sunday morning I went to the Elim Church in Armagh where my wife had been thriving and growing. I was only there a short time when I discovered why – beautiful people sharing a beautiful Saviour in a beautiful way and I was won over. That was to be my home and on the third Sunday Roberta and I capped it all by being baptised by Pastor John MacInnis. The blessing of obedience and the joy of witness combined to make it a day of strength and memories – the strength and memories I was going to need as I went back the following week to attend the start of my trial.

I felt like Paul leaving the Ephesians as I knelt with my family and prayed, cried and departed, heavy-hearted, and deeply hurt at the leaving. I then realised how hard it was going to be to go back, and how I needed God to give me the stamina and grit to do so. I did and was greatly disappointed to have our trial adjourned. I was remanded in custody again for six weeks. One thing led to another and our case kept being put back and what was meant to be a return to face trial was a return for another prison sentence of six weeks. I was devastated, and yet was able to recover on the strength of my memories of the three weeks and call to remembrance the things God had taught me. My baptism verse had been *"Fear thou not, for I am with thee, be not dismayed for I am thy God, I will strengthen thee, yea I will help thee, yea I will uphold thee with the right hand of my righteousness"* Isaiah 41 verse 10. How true! How true! For during the next six weeks a prison officer was murdered, industrial action took place, and hopes were dashed as delay followed delay. Upheld in the many arms of prayer I sought to witness and work amongst the needy in prison and in that six weeks shared my cell with individuals who came to hear and believe the Gospel – it surely was for a purpose.

# Chapter 14

# The Trial

My barrister, prior to the trial in June, gave it to me straight, "If things go well, we'll get you three to four years, but expect more." This was no shock to me. Derek's four years for what appeared trivial acts brought into stark reality the impending threat to our long term freedom. All the references possible were prepared. All the excuses possible were proffered, but who could deny the seriousness of my offences? Kidnapping, firearms offences etc., and all whilst a police sergeant – what excuse could there be? I was having great problems justifying myself. What would the judge say?

On that morning I awoke early, wondering how I had managed to sleep at all. I committed my day to the Lord and said, "Lord, not my will but Thine be done", but hoped that my will might be His too. I pictured myself in prison uniform and prayed that it might be brown (brown was for under three years, black for over three years). I didn't have breakfast in case I had something in my stomach to be sick over. I had a strange peace and felt very few nerves. The three of us were now together and encouraged each other. Prison officers wished us "the best of luck" as we passed them.

For the umpteenth time we crossed under the Crumlin Road through that old stone damp tunnel with its heating pipes leaking. What a march that was, but we knew it would be our last.

As I walked into the Court I saw a mass of faces, loved ones in one area, police in another, our Barristers on one side, the Prosecution's on the other. Black robes and white wigs abounded. Prison officers were behind and at the side of us. Jack and Willy had already received the sentences for their activities but Willy was with us for his part in ours. Those on bail were also with us and we all sat in stern-faced silence as the prosecution outlined the case against us. We had all pleaded guilty and all that remained was to be the defence's plea for mitigation. My plea for leniency was based upon my excellent record of courageous Police service, coupled with my misled but sincere motives to bring about an end to violence. Violence to end violence, pathetic but not malicious – the scene of young policemen exposed to ruthless prolonged and intensive terrorism, giving in to the desire to take the law into their own hands. This particular young policeman with four children, holder of the Queen's Gallantry Medal and Police commendations and now a born-again Christian, surely deserved some understanding and clemency!! Different people spoke on my behalf, including the Presbyterian chaplain who gave a very moving testimony to the, what he termed, real move of God in my life. When all was done the judge adjourned the case for consideration and we were led to the cells below.

Again, I felt no undue nerves. I felt strong and believed a true reflection had been drawn in respect of our past offences. We all talked around each others predicament but waited for what seemed an eternity before we were called back.

Lord Chief Justice Lowry proceeded to give his thoughts and from the very first sentence my hopes began to soar as he seemed to be trying to rationalise the irrational and justify the unjustifiable. Although he never for one moment condoned the acts, he looked compassionately on the actors and accepted the tremendous pressure we had been under. Before he ever got to the stage of passing sentence, I excitedly nudged Barry and said, "He's going to let us out!" Sure enough, against all the predictions and to the amazement of prosecution and defence, he gave us all suspended sentences for our acts of terrorism. None of us would serve any prison sentence. We were free! Without any thought and quite loud, I shouted, "Praise the Lord" only to be nudged by Barry who felt that such outbursts of heavenly joy should be from within at the best of times.

What a joyous occasion that was when we all shook hands with Officers and Defence and were madly embraced by weeping loved ones and overjoyed friends. The nightmare was over, the dream was carrying on. For a long time I basked in the blessing of being set free and wondered if it was true. In the middle of the corridor with others in Crumlin Road High Court, we all held hands and prayed a prayer of thanks for God's ultimate supernatural deliverance and rejoiced in being together again.

I went home to start my life again – unemployed, disgraced, embarrassed – but glory to God, free to start again.

After the initial revival of being out of prison for good and after all the handshakes and backclaps had disappeared or fallen away, I started the long haul back to respectability. To some I was a hero, to others a villain, but most importantly to my family, I was a husband and a father at home and I vowed to glorify God in my home and in my life.

Within weeks I was giving my testimony to God's saving grace in churches all over Ulster and was soon in a demand that I could not satisfy. I rejoiced in every opportunity to tell my friends of the great things God had done for me and as the redeemed of the Lord to "say so".

Monday mornings were the worst. By agreement, for security purposes, I had to sign on at the Unemployment Exchange. Sometimes I would go in the morning, sometimes in the afternoon, but whenever it was, I found it a most disagreeable thing. I hated it and longed for an opportunity to be employed again. I would stand in a queue amongst strangers, the only thing uniting us was our lack of a job, but surely most others would have been amazed if they knew my circumstances. Little did I know but some more sinister elements did.

It later transpired, and was declared in Court, that I had been followed, photographed, and set up to be murdered whilst attending the Unemployment Exchange. The man who set it up was convicted, a man involved in the conspiracy was also convicted, and the gunman who was to do the shooting died before he could carry out the act. He was shot dead by the Security Forces in a terrorist incident.

My mind went back to the threats made against me in prison, and as I considered, rejoiced over, and marvelled in God's providential care and protecting love, I wondered why I should have survived the type of action that so many better people than I had fallen victim to. God had promised to be with me on that baptismal Sunday morning, and had performed that which He had promised.

As I looked at the small army of terrorists in the court that day as I gave evidence against some of them, I was proving God's word in my life — no matter how vicious, well trained or dedicated these terrorists were, "if God was for me who could be against me?" The time was not right.

# Chapter 15
# Since Those Days

I went into full-time service with the Teen Challenge Organisation in Belfast, starting an operation called Prison Challenge, seeking to help in a practical and spiritual way prisoners and their families in need, providing clothes, money, transport, and evenings of Gospel Entertainment; seeing some saved, some set on their way and others just helped.

In 1982 I went to England and started a job as manager in a bedroom furniture factory. Mr. Watson was the first man who took me at face value and gave me an opportunity no-one else would. I will always be grateful for his trust.

I joined a small Evangelical Church and set up home. We became a part of the community. Our move to England became permanent. Things had moved at breakneck pace as prison brought freedom; freedom brought exposure to danger; danger brought a move to England; and England brought stability.

My wife and children enjoyed with me the new surroundings and we proved the total fallacy that English people are cold and withdrawn. We found new, deep and lasting friendships that proved unequivocally that those who are drawn to Christ, will be drawn together.

My children, especially Michelle and Adelle, came to terms with a world without the violence and terrorism that had numbed their minds and had made them so indifferent to its devastating effects.

England was to play a big part in my children breaking free from the bondage of Ulster's troubles, and they revelled in the freedom.

I threw myself into the work of the small, but effective, Emmanuel Evangelical church, and grew quickly under the tremendous Bible teaching of Pastor Cunningham.

I moved through the role of deacon to hold the position of elder – I believe, a role appointed by God. *"For the steps of a man made good are ordered by the Lord"* (my version). Very few here knew my background. I was neither a hero nor a villain, just Gary Armstrong – a Christian.

In the second part of the book I will share some of the lessons I have learned through my life and trust that you can draw something from them.

# PART II

## Chapter 1

# This Requires Some Urgency

I have told you before of the incidents that became normal routine in my life and in my duty as a policeman. Bomb scares typified the two extremes in terms of danger and response. Was the car abandoned outside the High Street shops packed with explosives purposed to maximise damage and thus maximise most economical hardship? Or was it a hoax meant to divert the Security Forces from attending to other activities? Or to cause maximum inconvenience and make another mark in the war of attrition? No-one ever knew until it either exploded or was cleared, but the response to the bomb scare was always the same for me. I had seen too many go off to take any chances and so, although at the back of my mind I thought to myself "this is a waste of time" – "late tea tonight" – "miss the rugby training today!", I knew that I had to react with the utmost urgency!

The best example I can think of was the one I referred to in Lurgan. John and I arrived with the accustomed mixture of "is it"? or "isn't it"? feelings, to the Chinese Restaurant. Our alcohol-provoked amusement at the hysteria and panic from the Chinese proprietors became the most sober and grave reaction, as we diagnosed that this **Was No Hoax**! It was for real – it looked real; the fertiliser mixture with plastic explosive from which the detonator protruded clearly stood out. It sounded real – the clock, just an ordinary alarm clock with bells ticked out its ominous countdown for destruction. It smelt real; pungent diesel soaked fertiliser, sure to add flames to explosive chaos. No mistaking it – IT WAS A BOMB AND IT WAS GOING TO EXPLODE.

Hearts pounding, adrenalin flowing, voices screeching, arms waving – all combined to ensure the desired effect – **people were to be directed to safety.** Self-preservation comes second as duty and training automatically combine to make sure the innocent neighbours are aroused from their sleep and informed of the grave danger they are in. Into action goes the well rehearsed but never perfect procedures of diverting traffic, sealing off the area and clearing it. It was of paramount importance to ensure the safety of the people, to the secondary importance of protecting property. When the bomb goes off and the building is demolished, no-one (apart from the mourning Chinese), appears too concerned. You see no-one has died or been injured – such was not always the case, as the record of carnage had proven.

During my short time as a Christian I have had tremendous conflict and difficulty in coming to terms with my lethargy and indifference in sharing the life-saving message of the Lord Jesus. In those times when I have mastered myself and realised the grave danger my fellow countrymen and women were in, (in terms of eternal destruction), I have continued to have great difficulty in wondering why I am one of so few who understand the times and what must be done. (Yes, I too forget my fickleness). The one thing that is more true today than in those days when my Lord walked on the earth is PEOPLE ARE IN REAL DANGER AND MOST OF THEM ARE UNAWARE OF THE TIME BOMB OF ETERNITY ABOUT TO EXPLODE IN THEIR FACES in the form of death or the return of the Lord. THEY MUST BE TOLD AND LED TO SAFETY.

I never argued with the residents in a danger area – If they didn't move I moved them. I didn't ask their religion; I didn't discuss the possibilities; I didn't allow them to finish off watching News at Ten – DANGER LURKED BUT SAFETY BECKONED.

I have never ceased to feel that I have achieved much on those all too few occasions when I have conveyed the reality of the danger to the people and they have readily run to the place of refuge. As the watchman I have enjoyed, but never gloated over, the opportunity to lead someone to Christ and eternal safety. I come back to earth as the ratio goes from "one to safety", to "fifty to death". I don't believe I have ever been preached into a realisation that the time is short, the jaws of hell are engulfing and I need to be redeeming the opportunities – I just know that it's true and have got to motivate myself to act upon my knowledge.

It seems to me that too many are too willing to see the danger, content in the fact of their own safety, and only alert others if the programme of evangelism allows it and the church leaders have authorised it. Surely duty and training must combine to make it a natural response when we see so many in danger of going to a place of eternal punishment, to seek to pluck them as *"brands from the burning"*?

I have come to the conclusion that I would be so much more effective if I enjoyed and relished my job as a bomb warden. If I revelled in the task of leading and ushering many to safety I would feel so much more in tune with the mind and heart of Christ. Oh, to serve the Lord with gladness, and yet regardless of my feelings my duty is clear, and sound the alert I will – abounding in the times when the love of Christ provokes me and the plight of people draws me, and abiding in the times when it is a matter of *"Not my will but Thine be done"*.

As a servant of Christ I have no option but to obey and warn the wicked – I have no alternative as a watchman of the Lord but to *"Cry aloud and spare not"*. I have striven and pressed towards the mark of being a willing and enthusiastic servant of Christ, and I don't know about you, but I find that objective always near but yet so far. If there are many or any of you who have attained to that objective, realising the danger, alerting the unheeding and unaware, and abounding in the true joy of doing it – please encourage me and others who are looking to that end. To those who have failed to realise the danger that others are in, never having set out to warn them, be warned yourself *"his blood I will require at thine hand"*.

# Chapter 2

# Judgement

In our land today and probably throughout most of the affluent Western world, there appears to be a pathetic perception of "what lies ahead". As General Booth, the founder of the Salvation Army, established in the early days of this once great organisation – people need to get a vision of hell and all that it entails to inspire them to the degree of urgency that the apostate world requires today.

Such was the case with me as I moved from the abounding and energetic throes of my conversion. In prison after my conversion I was desperately conscious of the need to witness to my great salvation and to my wonderful Saviour. Full of youthful exuberance in the Lord, it was no hardship to use my visits to invite my former friends and my relatives to a "Gospel Service" they couldn't escape from. I used my five letters per week to evangelise acquaintances, comrades and relatives. The success or otherwise of those letters will be an eternal measurement but I always felt that letter writing, as Paul would testify, was as powerful a tool as any. I threw myself into evangelism within the prison and always found willing listeners as well as unwilling sceptics.

This motivation and inspiration continued long after I came out of prison and into my new church life and ministry to the prisoners and their families, via Prison Challenge, and to young people through the Lighthouse in Dungannon. Often duty was more a factor than unadulterated love for the lost, but the Lord honoured the work I was involved in.

Yet, time, familiarity and preoccupations have succeeded from time to time to deprive me of that vision of the end of the people whose God is not the Lord – THE FEARFUL EXPECTATION OF JUDGEMENT.

In an attempt to illustrate the horror and desperation facing the man or woman who has not been born again, I have often thought of my journey through the legal process and courts and I see a real parallel to the journey the vast majority of people are taking – life!

It began when I was arrested and my house was searched. The legal process that began that day would one day end up in a court before the highest and most senior judge in the country. Questioning followed, statements were made, and at a special court I was charged with criminal offences. I pleaded "Not Guilty" – intent on beating the rap by foul or fair means – in my case it had to be foul. Over months of weekly remand appearances my defence worked on the "Way Out" – and how I wrestled with the situation – making excuses – looking for loopholes and expecting a miracle worker called a "Barrister" to talk me to freedom. I knew I was guilty, but guilty men had got off before! Even after I had given my life to the Lord I found it so difficult to let go of the desire to wriggle my way out of the mess. Arraignment was next and our plea of guilty was lodged and our hearing was put back to allow other cases to be concluded.

Finally one day I, with my guilty colleagues, stood in front of the top judge – grim faced and wig clad. The court was full of barristers, lawyers, police, spectators and of course defendants. The prosecution outlined the sorry case against me, sparing no facts and allowing no favours. My defence counsel then pleaded on my behalf, citing my bravery, my dedication, the pressure I worked under etc. etc. A minister in Crumlin Road spoke on my behalf.

Then all the talking stopped and the Judge spoke. He adjourned the Hearing and we awaited our sentence. My stomach heaved, my hands and legs shook with nerves, my lips were dry and perspiration broke as I anticipated my sentence.

I was called with my fellow defendants. I stood before the Judge. Nothing more could be said on my behalf, nothing could be said by me, the only one who could speak was the Judge and no-one could interrupt him or question him. He finally pronounced his judgement!

This is where the comparison, feeble and inappropriate as it is, ends for the unsaved one. His life will be searched by the all-seeing eye of God, nothing can be hidden. Excuses may be offered and escape routes sought for avoiding the judgement, but there is no escape once the Great Judge pronounces His judgement on those who have neglected or rejected Him.

His inevitable sentence to the guilty ones, who will have nothing to say, will be to send them to the most indescribably awful and injurious place beyond the most vivid imagination of men. *"Depart from Me, ye cursed"*.

I have heard many descriptions of hell but I must confess they all fall short of what I believe it must truly be. Just as eye hasn't seen, nor ear heard, nor has the heart conceived, the things that God has prepared for those who love Him – comparatively eye, ear nor heart, cannot conceive the things which God has prepared for those who don't. It is beyond our comprehension when we consider the wars with their tortuous ends; the inhumanity displayed throughout the generations; the earthquakes; the famines; the diseases; the persecutions etc. etc. Humanity has seen and conceived the most awful things – but no eye has seen, no ear heard, no heart conceived what the Lord has prepared for those who do not love Him.

It is to that background that I, as a Christian, by way of reminder and disciplined approach, must continue to keep hell before me and act as a barrier, a signpost and a diversion, to those who would seek its occupation.

To those who are not yet children of the Lord I ask them to do as I did and plead their guilt, before death and judgement come, for to enter death pleading innocence will not avail. God is seeking the sick, not the healthy – God is calling the guilty and not the innocent. His acceptance of you as a guilty sinner this side of eternity is just as sure as His rejection of you, unrepentant on the other side.

# Chapter 3

# Unfulfilled Potential

Within our natural world can be found the natural remedies for some of our greatest plagues and diseases – cancer, leukaemia etc., but no-one as yet has been able to tap the resources and combine them to the right measure to effect a cure for unfulfilled potential!

One night I was at the scene of an incident when a bomb was planted outside the door of a Roman Catholic owned pub. A five gallon tin had been packed with gelignite and a fused detonator. Shots had been fired from machine guns and handguns to introduce the arrival of the gang who proceeded to plant the bomb at the door of the pub. Having shot one man they fled the scene to allow their bomb to go off, causing maximum injury and devastation. The fuse had been lit.

The fact is that the bomb failed to go off because only the detonator exploded – not the bomb! The plan had gone wrong and the purpose was thwarted because the bomb failed to explode – unfulfilled potential.

One of the great tragedies of the contemporary church is that it, generally, is a saga of "unfulfilled potential" stories. I have too many beams in my own eyes to pick the motes out of the churches, but it is with great sadness that I have recoiled time after time in the face of the selfish, political and fleshly antics of the church – diverted from its called task and causing only hell and the devil to rejoice.

In my short time as a Christian I have seen churches and outreaches grow from nothing, as a grain of mustard seed, to be mighty weapons of evangelism in the hand of the Lord and just as quickly fall apart into semi-retirement and ineffectual ministry. Why? Because people thought more of themselves that they ought; because lust for power and covetousness of other people's talents quenched the fire and spoilt the potential. Don't blame the devil, he didn't need to get involved, the fleshly antics of pride-filled and power-hungry people was quite enough.

Thus the church becomes schismatic and divided, and though I don't seek a united church where respectable uniformity paralyses the Spirit's spontaneity, I must confess that I see within the local and widespread church of today, certainly in the West, a great unfulfilled potential.

Talented men and women, energetic boys and girls are crippled as the natural overwhelms the spiritual and apathy, indifference and indolence take over. Some years ago I was privileged to visit the Grand Canyon, but what a bitter disappointment it was to me (give me Yosemite any day). It is a rapidly decaying monument to the destructive forces of nature! What is described as one of the great wonders of the world is a crumbling mass of stone and clay – collapsing before the combined forces of wind and water.

This is how I see the church today. From the outside it looks a magnificent object of human endeavour and God's pleasure, when for the most part it is disintegrating and becoming a memorial to what used to happen but somehow today isn't – collapsing before the combined forces of worldliness and materialism.

I know there are the exceptions but the Church is largely impotent in stopping the onward surge of materialism, worldliness, immorality and ungodliness, and in some instances in the vanguard of such an onslaught!

I have had the privilege of speaking in almost every denomination in Ulster and what I say to them I say to myself – who is winning the war for the loyalty and allegiance of the people? It is not what we say – it is what we are, and if Christ is not seen in us He is not seen. I love the fundamentalism of the Free Presbyterians; I love the "priesthood of all Believers" emphasis of the Brethren; I love the dynamic worship of Elim; I love the Church government set up in the Baptists etc. etc., but I long for each to fulfil its potential and make an impact in its own area of responsibility. If we all could explode with the dunamis power that God has promised to those who desire, value and utilise it, then we surely can destroy the principalities and pull down the strongholds: Pious platitudes? Like the early Church I know that He can do what He has said, and anyway what is the alternative – to whom can we go?

I thank God for the day He lit the fuse in my life. I further thank Him for the night He exploded the detonator and granted me the power and desire to witness – how I long for the bomb to wreak havoc to the principalities and powers around me. Pride and prejudice, exclusivity and speciality, shallowness of doctrine and broadness of practice, tolerance of the forbidden and intolerance of the permitted, are all ingredients to ensure the explosion does not take place. Couple that with the personal lack of application of God's people and you will understand why the broad road is choc-a-bloc and the narrow road is crowd free.

The most powerful ingredients to instigate the necessary explosion can be found throughout the third world i.e. simplicity, childlike faith, lack of materialism and unrespectability in the eyes of authorities. I confess the price for me is a tremendous one to pay, but I need not wonder why there is no explosion – just a series of pops, hoaxes and unexploding bombs – "unfulfilled potential."!!

# Chapter 4

# **Good Intentions**

It is said that good intentions pave the way for bitter disappointments. I am sure I am in a huge majority when I say my life has been a series of good intentions, from the days when I intended to set myself a revision schedule in school, follow it rigidly, work hard and pass my exams, until the day in which I now write this chapter, having promised it would have been started days before now.

The danger of the philosophy of good intentions is that the failure to make good the intention can be written off as an innocuous lapse or an excusable detour – "Something distracted me" – "I had to do something more important" – "I can do it any time" – some more convenient time!

In retrospect and as I examine my own failures, I am sure that there are many excuses for our failures to secure our intentions, but only one reason – the deceitfulness of our hearts i.e. our ability to cheat ourselves and others and then somehow excuse the whole affair with a commonly used and probably widely accepted excuse.

One of the best examples of such a broken promise and the cost attached to the failure to make good on it, was the incident when I went to the Isle of Man on a boat with my terrorist friends. Most of you will be able to associate with the thoughts that permeated my mind at that time, but the intention of relating it is not to encourage you to believe you are one of many, but that you might understand the grave consequences and the unacceptable standards of "telling lies" and disguising them as good intentions just forgotten. It is not on, to pass failure off as an abortive new resolution, or a new leaf falling back. Accept that you have cheated your soul, and more importantly, the great Creator of it.

It was a really good day as we, a band of loyal fighters, opted out of the cut and thrust of Ulster's terror situation and enjoyed a day at the races, the Isle of Man T.T. We had left Kilkeel early in the morning and by midday were in situ looking eagerly at the flashing machinery with human pilots throwing themselves at incredible speed into corners and awaiting eagerly the prospect of some of them throwing themselves off at incredible speed to our morbid satisfaction. The day passed quickly and I had no thought whatsoever for the journey home. Well, the captain had got us over safely and it was just a reverse journey, so when we set off to pick up the boat in the early afternoon I had no notion of what lay ahead.

The wind had got up but I wouldn't have noticed that but for a comment made in passing as we made our way to the port, that a storm was in the air. Yet, by the time we had reached the port I was just a little concerned as a right mini storm was whipping up. It quickly grew into much concern when I heard the experienced boatmen discuss the possibility of staying on the Isle of Man until the winds died down, but I must admit my ignorance of the whole art of sailing, effect of winds etc., made my contribution one of sham courage and sublime indifference. The fact that no-one knew we were in the Isle of Man; we had no radio, no life jackets, no flares, one small outboard motor without a backup etc., made the situation ideal for a pragmatic evaluation and a graceful retreat to the safety of an Isle of Man tavern. The only conviction I had was not to be a coward but if faced with a choice I should go for the hard one, especially if the captain and leader was going for that one too. The truth of the matter, as I believe in so many of the foolish ventures that shower our history, was that no-one wanted to say "No" and therefore the absence of opposition was stronger than the presence of resolve.

Off we went with each passing moment elevating the strength of the wind and the intensity of the storm. The writing on our defiant wall was plain for all to see as it took us half an hour to get clear of the port. The plea to return to the Isle's port was probably the loudest unspoken plea I have ever made because I was getting very nervous about the whole exploit. Unfortunately no-one did anything positive for fear of being accused of being negative, and as we reached the point of no return we all realised that our cowardice was more evident in setting off than having the courage of our convictions to stay (surely this can be mirrored in many of the terrorist acts that happen in our world today – a seed is sown – an act is nurtured and when the weed is seen it is allowed to grow when everyone knows it should be uprooted).

I was now definitely and unashamedly scared and unafraid to say so – how pathetic I must have been as I came face to face with the reality of a stormy sea which, depending on its appetite, would within hours either swallow me or spit me up. The odds were all pointing to being swallowed. Things might have been less intimidating if someone, anyone, had said something optimistic but everyone was scared stiff and no-one could see the little motor boat with overworked motor, tossed as a leaf to and fro on wicked and immense waves ever making the near but yet so very far place of safety.

Thinking only the worst and gradually losing any hope of making it, I did what every other person with a divinely placed Spirit would do – I cried unto the Lord by reason of my affliction – a real Jonah! "Lord, if I come out of this" (which of course means, Lord, make sure you get me out of this) "I will be a different person from what I have been. I will value my family, I will go to my church, I will be a nicer person". Isn't it unchanging that in a time of threat and danger our thinking occupies family, church, and self? But I honestly meant it. I realised, as I reeled from one side of the matchbox cabin to the other and assumed the most penitent and humbling position before God as the storm would allow, that I had been a very selfish, empty, ungodly person and the apparent imminence of death by drowning (as I thought) was crystallizing some very real issues in my life. My little girl's faces flashed repeatedly before me; my wife's love and dedication endeavoured to combat the cold, uncaring elements and I genuinely wanted another chance to show I could appreciate them. If let off the "hook" my life and values would change and no-one would fail to notice. "Lord, this is a one sided contract – only you can win – I'll give you all for one little insignificant act of life-saving."

The reaching of the harbour in Ulster did nothing to take away from the real sense of escape. I wasn't going to forget the experience and I was going to be different as a result. My intentions were not only good but as good as done!

The next day I played with the children and took my wife to her mother's. I had already begun to honour my side of the bargain, although I wondered, as I reflected, if I had not over-reacted and perhaps the storm was not as bad after all, and it was just my inexperience that made it seem so awful.

I went to church the next Sunday and made a real effort to listen the whole way through. Well, it did go the whole way through – in one ear and out the other.

Very soon I was preoccupied once again with my dual standard lifestyle and before long my good intentions, like so many before, had become just mere intentions. I once again took my wife for granted and spent little time with my children. Church only beckoned when nothing more important like a lie-in did! I had convinced myself by neglect of commitment to my promise that my deliverance from death was merely a panic stricken mind temporarily losing its bearings and sera sera – what was meant to be, was!

The vast majority of people will not have been faced with the same particular situation as that portrayed, but you will associate with a time in your own experience when you have resolved to respond to the good and right nature somewhere within and began to turn the tables on the status quo. Invariably there has been a spiritual dimension – not, I must give up smoking; not, I must not be late for work; **but**, I must change my lifestyle, do things differently and be less self-styled and selfish.

We do ourselves a great disservice when we commit ourselves to something and fail to go through with it, not by reason of inability for that would be perhaps noble, but by reason of disinclination. What seems the right thing to do one moment, is not as attractive the next and our fickle minds and hearts forego the right and positive way.

We may be Christian and we vow to spend more time in prayer, or at Bible Study, for we know it is right, but there is something dreadfully wrong when we can, with so little recrimination, give up or relax on the commitment. In doing so we reduce our effectiveness and chip just one more little stone out of the wall of our Christian Jerusalem on the road to a ruined replica of what "might have been". Do we really consider the damage done to our spiritual nature by every reneged commitment – one step forward and two steps back means reverse in any man's language!

We may be non-Christian and we vow to give time and activity to pursuing an interest in our family or our neighbours or most beneficially in our God, but the storm ceases and the need for a fulfilment of the commitment is not as important. It is soon overwhelmed, buried and extinguished by more, relatively speaking, important issues. Do you not realise the harm being done to that potentially awakening spirit within you, as it is chloroformed into sleep again by the absence of your resolve to go through with what you have promised?

The blatant, unpalatable and inexcusable truth of the matter, whoever we are, is that we all fall short on that attainable but hard won goal of saying what we mean, and meaning what we say and doing what we have promised. Quickened consciences and sensitive minds will not rest or relax until that which has been purposed has been performed and the individuals performing their purpose are bound to be richer and fuller as a result.

If you need, like the Philippian jailer, an earthquake; or if, like Jonah, you need a storm, then you can be sure God's love is strong enough to shake you from the terminal status quo. His power is sufficient to enable you to go through and pay your vows — your storm or earthquake awaits you.

# Chapter 5

# **Bridge That Gap**

Since becoming a Christian some twelve years ago, one very real difference noticed by most of those who know me well has been that I am much more content than I was before. Godliness and contentment has been great gain to me. If there is one ingredient missing in the lives of our generation today above all others it is "contentment".

Today I am quite happy to be at home with my family or to be on holiday with them. I am just as content now in watching the local school play rugby, as in playing it myself (although I miss the physical aspect). Such was not always the case and I believe for many such is not the case.

From my earliest days at home as a child I had to be doing something different. I would get fed-up with the way I had my fort built and I would have to knock it down and make a shop! A few days later I would be trying out the fishing rod – caught nothing. I would once again try to get that plastic bottle right between the posts as I converted the winning try to seal the match. Well, it's part of growing up isn't it? Or is it?

You see, when I grew up nothing seemed to change. In the S.P.G. pursuits abounded but none of them seemed to satisfy. I wasn't content at home so I tried to fill the gap with work – "The O.T. King" I used to be called. Sure, I liked the money but I needed the work. Darts gave way to cards, to pool, to boobytrapping colleagues' lockers etc. etc. Interests in crazy paving lasted momentarily and turned to D.I.Y. which lasted less time. Satisfaction and contentment beckoned but never materialised. I thought I had cracked it with the rugby winter time and cricket summer time, but they left me even more dissatisfied because the immense satisfaction in playing was too temporal and the anti-climax was so real – I couldn't play rugby every day all day!

Socialising was never a priority but as I searched for something to fill the gap, it beckoned me and I tasted it to see what it was like. Always proving to be a means of spending time it never proved to be a fulfilling means of redeeming it. Performing the party piece, or fighting the piece out – I, like so many beside me, was merely going through the motions of routine, and as the suicides in the police were to prove, availability of pursuits and recreational activity were no guarantee of attaining satisfaction with life.

I suppose my flutter with drugs, and to a more intense degree my involvement in terrorism, were further clues to the fact that I was being consumed by the nothingness of it all and, as a disturbed mouse, I was scurrying helterskelter to find the answer.

Money couldn't buy it – for new cars, new homes, new clothes, new entertainment venues, could not satisfy.

Reputation couldn't earn it – for having an unbeaten fight record, having a top performance on duty award, having a Queen's Gallantry Medal, still could not satisfy.

Family couldn't provide it – four beautiful, endearing children, a loving and loyal wife, a caring and interested family circle, were vanity in satisfaction terms.

Recreation couldn't give it – for football, rugby, cricket, darts, snooker etc., all fell abysmally short in the satisfaction stakes.

Church couldn't answer it – for Sunday School, Boy's Brigade, C.L.B., and Church Services, left me void of satisfaction promised.

You see, all of the above in themselves were valuable stocking fillers, but none of them were the principle and primary present! I found on the 21st December 1978 that the Lord Jesus was not only the answer to my search for satisfaction and contentment – He was satisfaction and contentment. When He became a part of me so did they – just free with the main offer! He didn't bridge the gap, He did away with it! He didn't provide the missing link, He broke the chain and threw it away! I live, yet not I, He lives in me and His life in me produces the fruit that all my searching, testing, and working could never do – the inevitable stream from the invincible Source.

Now confession time! The always evident "old man" fights to make dissatisfaction and discontentment a reality in my experience of life. See if you can tick off any of the following in your life, as I demonstrate I am not ignorant of his devices.

1. I am not satisfied with the way the church is being run. The pastors carry too much power and the Church body ministry is curtailed. The church needs changing.

2. I am not content with the way the evangelism outreaches are being run. There is not enough practical outreach.

3. I am dissatisfied with the worship service – not enough life – too much Pastoral input, not enough spontaneity.

   And so it goes on. You fill in your favourite moan or grouse.

Criticism is the greatest evidence of a discontented heart and usually is the chief means in bringing it about. Judgement of others is necessary but only possible when it has begun with ourselves and more often will be unspoken when such an introspection is undertaken. "I have learned to be content –" said Paul and I am also learning. Just as at school, it wasn't easy to learn, and required discipline and hard work, so it is today in learning to be content and allowing Christ to have His way in our lives.

Perhaps others who read this do not have any worries about God or Church because they don't feature, but you're honest enough to see and say that your life is a saga of unfulfilled ambitions, disappointments, empty antics and searching for the invisible. You can relate to me as I tried so many different methods to hit the jackpot only to find there is no lasting satisfaction. You may feel that this is the way life is meant to be – You're a "life executive" jet hopping from one experience to another, never supposed to reach a final destination nor a place of restful fulfilment.

Let me assure you, as a result of my experience of chasing the wind, you can attain contentment, the degree depending on how well you are learning, and you can be satisfied; but I promise you it can only be found in a relationship with the person of the Lord Jesus Christ. You need not let your disappointments or failures be sinking sand but stepping stones and a propellant to get you to the point where you will say – "Lord Jesus, in You, let my satisfaction be found".

A knowledge that God knows our frame and the things we have need of, is the starting point. A simple child-like dependence on Him coupled with a commonsense and Biblically directed approach to the affairs of life will cultivate and produce the much sought after, seldom-achieved, fruit of contentment. Deep down you know it to be so.

I remember when we were looking for the body of a Protestant businessman in South Armagh, kidnapped, bestially tortured and murdered by the I.R.A., we spent days looking in derelict houses on the border. During these searches we were fired on from across the border by I.R.A. snipers. Some days later his body was found many miles from where we had been concentrating our efforts. All that danger to ourselves, and all the time his body was far away.

Many people are today concentrating their efforts to find peace, satisfaction and content-ment in the wrong places and at considerable danger to themselves. Are Aids, lung cancer, car accident deaths from speed and alcohol, drug overdoses, suicides etc., not irrefutable evidence that there is an incredible risk in searching in the wrong places. If we had known where to find the body a lot of time and resources would have been saved and a lot of danger evaded.

Let me point you to where the answer and the end of your searching is: THE LORD JESUS CHRIST.

# Chapter 6

# As For Me

I am sure, once again, that I form part of the majority when I admit that for most of my life I found it difficult to go against the crowd or to swim against the current.

From the days when at school a group of us, "The Gang", would go to the cinema and smoke like chimneys, even though none of us liked it but it was the thing to do, and no-one wanted to curb the adventure.

To the days when we would dress up in "Mufties" (civilian coat over our police uniform) and abscond from duty to a party or dance, parking the police car in a garage and taking off into the night – everyone knowing the risks but taking them rather than be labelled killjoys.

To the day when rather than be the oddball, I would take my first alcoholic beverage, hating every taste, but just to be one of the boys!

Right up to the day when confronted with a choice to embark upon a crazy scheme to kidnap Father Murphy at Ahoghill rather than be branded a coward to the cause; I chose to once again go along rather than have the courage to question my motives.

During my time in prison I had the opportunity to talk with terrorists who had been caught, or on remand, and I learnt a fact that all too often is denied. The vast majority of young men in prison are there not because they were willing volunteers to terrorist acts, but unwilling conscripts without the courage or will to say no. Get a group of young men with a common value and watch them string along until it's out of hand and too late to pull out. We are all accountable for our actions and must pay the price for making wrong choices, but who can deny that whether in a terrorist act, football-hooliganism, door-knocking, shop looting, pub crawling etc., most people find it easier to say YES when it is better to say NO.

All over the world movements carry people along until the momentum is the physical force, and not principles or objectives. Atrocities, wars, crime abound when individuals compromise the knowledge of right to play their part in the crowd and do wrong. To a greater or lesser degree it must be true of us all at some stage.

Things changed for me when I became a Christian, and suddenly and continuously I found that the word "NO" when spoken in love is a powerful positive in a very negative world. As I read through the Scriptures I found out for myself that through a body functioning as such, the individual members had unique roles which not only should not be copied by other members, but must not. I was very struck by the Lord's almost cutting answer to Peter when He asked what would happen to John in John 21, only to be told "What is that to thee?" In other words, don't worry what others should do, concentrate on what you must do. Paul did not say, "Lord, what would You have them to do?", but, "What would you have **me** to do?" It is "As for **me**" not "As for you". I learnt that because the broad way that led to destruction contained many and the narrow way contained few, I would of necessity find myself more often than not moving against the majority view, and even though it would be difficult, I was going to have to be my own man, or more precise, God's man on his own.

Sometime after coming out of prison I was put to the test as never before on my avowed principle of proving all things, and then doing what I felt was right regardless of the reaction. Being involved with prisoners and their families, I was approached by a man who was introducing Prison Fellowship to Ulster. I was encouraged to go to America and to see for myself the work of Prison Fellowship and meet its founder Chuck Colson. I was sent on my way to spend three weeks. I reached the point where I was confronted with a choice of accepting an ecumenical arrangement which I disagreed with and thus offend no-one, or earnestly contend for the faith as I understood it, and refuse the offer. By adopting the first I would have kept my hosts, new friends and my sponsor happy and no-one need have known back home about it. I would have compromised a little but pleased a lot. By taking the latter course of action I would offend my host, my sponsor, my new friends, Mr. Colson, and would have to come home a week early as I knew I could not have stayed. It is history that I took the latter course, but it is historical that it was a battle within myself to make unpopular decisions and do what I believed to be right. I would like to think that I was sensitive and humble in following through my decision, and that has always been my desire. I found after that that I could make difficult decisions, explain them, and even when in a minority of one, stand by them. In my church in Northwich, during the Annual General Meetings I could never just go along with the vote for the purposes of peace and popularity. The secret in all of this was to be uncontentious. A gracious spirit would agree to disagree and continue to go forward. I still press to this end.

I find though that in the Church there is a bad connotation to the word "individual". The emphasis is on the "body" and on working as "a unit". the thrust of evangelism is organised as group outreaches. Seminars emphasise our integration within the church and the man or woman, boy or girl, is swallowed up by a large unit.

I am not saying as individual members we must not work together and compliment each other – for we do – I am just saying we are INDIVIDUAL MEMBERS. We must not be man pleasers; we must not govern our actions by what others think or say; we must not order our lives to accommodate the acceptable face of churchianity – we must be individuals! Independent assessment of situations will bring independent actions. Though men called by God to be leaders, pastors etc., have a vital role in directing, counselling and challenging us, it is the individual who is accountable to God for his actions. There must be church discipline and there must be accountability to God's ordained leadership but that does not disqualify individuality.

God is not churning us out on a conveyor belt programmed to act and react the same. Yet, in every church I have attended, people generally follow each other and the people who are prepared to be different are few and far between. So many look to their leaders, others to pre-eminent people in the church, others to famous or well-known personalities, still others to men of old whose biographies challenge even today, and others to biblical characters for inspiration and example.

Personally I too have been inspired by such, but more than ever I realise I must look to the Lord Jesus alone and through His Word I will find the principle portions of my doctrinal beliefs and witnessing practices complementing that of my brethren and sisters. I refuse to conform to any pattern that is not glaringly apparent to me as a result of looking unto Jesus, who is the author and finisher of my faith. Each man must be fully persuaded in his own mind.

Copycatting, blind obedience, uniform and routine performances have no place in the true Christian Church of today, but sadly predominate. Personal assessment, considered responses, constant evaluation and individualistic but body-complimenting activity will breathe a refreshing society-transforming breath of air through our country – an end to which we all could concur.

To participate in organised activity is one thing but to organise an activity to participate in is totally different. If I as an individual am prepared to act on my own, then I believe that I will be doing service as unto the Lord which will contribute to the Church's purpose of evangelising. There need not be conflict – there must be a will to *'do'*. The great Head of the body will still co-ordinate the actions of His members, and whilst on occasions will use all members together to perform a task, He will on occasions, just use one to do another task.

Be your own person – seek opportunities to do in secret what your Father in Heaven will see and reward, and be constantly minded that in all things you should see "JESUS ONLY".

# Chapter 7

# The Invitation
# of a Sovereign

I have already mentioned the receipt of my invitation from Her Majesty The Queen to attend Buckingham Palace to receive the Queen's Gallantry Medal.

I have tried previously to describe the absolute astonishment and undisguised delight that abounded in my heart and my home, when it dawned on me what had happened and was to happen. To be able to take my wife Roberta and my mother on this trip of a lifetime was a bonus indeed.

In this, my last chapter, I give a gospel allegory and show the sheer folly of rejecting the greatest invitation of all.

When I received the notification of my award and the invitation to go to the Palace and meet the Queen, I knew immediately that it was very, very important. You see, it carried the Royal Seal, and was clearly identified as being from a Royal source. The letter simply outlined my award and indicated where and when it should take place.

Initially I was bewildered, not knowing why I should be receiving such an honour and trying to work out what I'd done to receive it. When I came to terms with the invitation and importance of it, I was delighted that I, amongst others, should be chosen to receive it. I had known of others who had received medals from members of the Royal Family at Hillsboro Castle, but to go to the Palace and receive personally from the Queen herself, my medal, filled me with pride and joy.

The thrilling expectation and happy anticipation lasted for weeks as the day drew near. The medal was mine. It had been engraved with my name, but until the Queen handed it to me, it wouldn't be mine to have and to hold. With my colleagues, we made our preparations or had them made for us. The other aspect of the event was that it was free – it was going to cost me nothing. The flights were paid, the hotel was paid, the meals were paid, and I even got an allowance for going!

I had seen the Palace on a T.V. screen. I had seen the changing of the Guard with the immaculate Guardsmen performing so regally, but to be able to walk through the gates as many looked on, to walk within a yard of the Guardsmen and on into the Palace, was overwhelming and for the most part I was silently bemused.

In the Preparation Room I was given instructions how to respond to Her Majesty. I wanted to look immaculate. I made sure my cap peak shone, my boots also, and every loose hair was located and dealt with on my uniform. Physically, cosmetically, and mentally, I was ready.

To this day I cannot remember much of what happened in the Ceremony Room that day. My wife, whose memory has not diminished, has informed me of how regal and grand the whole scene was as she surveyed the Palace – its red and gold carpet, huge paintings covering large walls and beautiful antique furnishings with enormous crystal chandeliers.

We lined up to receive our awards and I cannot put in words my thoughts as Her Majesty entered and sat on her throne. By the time she, dressed in her pale blue dress and white gloves, adorned with pearls and wearing a diamond tiara, got to me I was a nervous wreck. I can't remember her words apart from the general – "Well done".

With my medal in my hands I floated out of the Palace to go through the photographic rituals and proudly display to all and sundry my prided possession. That day there were more famous people than I but none of us were treated any differently. It was indeed the experience of a lifetime.

Now to my allegory . . .

Imagine you receive in the post an invitation to go to the Palace and meet the Queen. How would you react? Push it onto the unpaid bills pile? Throw it in the bin? Put it away until another day? Or would you with joy gladly respond with a "Yes, I will come, immediately". The incredible thing is that many are hearing an invitation from the King of Kings today, and are treating it with disdain, contempt or indifference. Truly there is no reason why He should invite you, for you have done nothing to deserve it, nor is there any reason He should acknowledge you, never mind give you an expense paid, free of charge, trip to His royal place of abode (heaven, to those who need to know its name). Let me assure you that no act, or work you have done, could possibly earn the reward He has in store for those who love Him – for He just wants to give it to those who will receive it as a love gift from Him.

Even though it may be some time before you meet your King to physically receive your reward, it can be truly yours today for your name can be written on it, kept in store for that day when all will be unfolded. All the while you can live your life in joyful expectation of that meeting and be thrilled day by day by the thought that soon and very soon you will go to see the King – just because He loved you and sent His Son to invite you to share His royal eternity.

Nothing on earth you will ever see can compare with the regal splendour and untainted beauty of the place God has prepared for those that love Him and respond affirmatively to His invitation. Clues, insights, and vague images abound in the Bible, but of necessity the indescribable cannot be described and the eternal cannot be weighed in the minds of temporal beings. You don't even have to worry about your uniform. Just like mine it is provided by the Crown. A royal robe of righteousness is yours in exchange for your sin-stained black robes, dyed in rebellion and shameful resistance to the lawful King. Black became white when red was applied – the blood of the Lord Jesus can cleanse you from your sin and give you the garments in which you need not be afraid to stand before the King of Kings.

The book of Revelation gives a glimpse of the impact of the entry of the King upon all those gathered around the throne. Worship, adoration and adulation abound as He is recognised and revered by those who, with the eyes of faith and child-like simplicity, have beheld Him as their King of Glory and Prince of Peace. Hymnwriters, poets and prophets tried to describe the scene when the King is paraded before His adoring subjects in all His regal splendour and glorious victory. Such an entry was not the case as my Queen entered, but she has done nothing to merit such a reception unlike my King Jesus who has done all things so well in defeating the enemy and the devil. He dealt with the only thing that can stop you spending eternity with Him – SIN – yours, and mine – finally and eternally done for on the cross and affirmed by the resurrection.

How shall He be attired? I believe only glorified and new eyes can possibly behold the brilliance and purity of the appearance of the One whose vesture was once dipped in His own blood and upon whose head one crown could never be enough – it has to be many crowns!

What will He say to those who respond to His invitation to come? I believe He will say, "Well done", and eternity will record and echo the contrast with the words spoken to those who put the invitation aside until the R.S.V.P. date has passed – "Depart from Me". Which is it to be with you?

The allegory only suffices to draw your mind to the inescapable conclusion, that no person in their right mind could possibly resist or reject such an offer, to attend the most blessed of ceremonies in the home of the King of Kings. Sadly, many minds, mine being one were darkened for so long, so that the light was unable to shine in. Many hearts are hard so that invitations untouched by natural hands, from a King, unseen by natural eyes, relating to an eternity inconceivable to natural hearts, are brushed aside and lost in the insatiable abyss of lost opportunities. It is only when the natural assumes the spiritual, that there is triggered within the life of an individual the awareness that all is not well, and all will not be well should things continue unchanged.

The purpose of my book is to enable you to

objectively and comparatively analyse your life, past, present and future. Having performed this analysis it is hoped that there is sufficient help within the pages to point to the One who is able to do exceeding abundantly above all you can ask or even think. Such is His desire to effectually call you into His Kingdom and share with you the treasures of it, both now and in the future. Stark contrasts abound in the valley of decision and in the conflict of exiting such a valley having made the right decision. Heaven or hell, hope or despair, Christ or the devil, eternal life or eternal death and so on . . .

There is a choice and yet there is no choice. The fact that so many get it wrong indicates that it is neither an easy choice or an apparent choice. God has got to get us to the point where we realise that there is a choice, what the choice is and the consequences of the choice we make. My life, and that of millions of others, assure you that God is no respecter of persons and is not willing that you should make the wrong choice. For all of the inadequacies of this book, and for all the faults and failures of the writer of it, the one thing it says to every ear who will hear, is that God is in the business of calling people, changing people, preparing people and in doing all these, blessing people.

If you are able to hear, if you need to be changed, if you want to be prepared, and if you long to be blessed, then simply do the following: –

1. Acknowledge God to be the Great Creator and only true God.

2. Acknowledge your need to be reconciled to Him, your sin having separated you from Him.

3. Ask Him, through the finished work of His Son on Calvary and as a result of the shedding of His own blood, to forgive and cleanse you of your sin.

4. Call on Him as your Lord and Saviour and claim your right to be called His child.

5. Rejoice in your great salvation and worship the Lord for His total and absolute part in bringing it into being.

6. Tell others what He has done for you and what He can do for them.

7. Immerse yourself in His Word – learn – search – grow – meditate.

8. Communicate with Him who loved you and gave Himself for you – always.

9. Join a Church that makes their boast only in Jesus; honours His Word and offers you a loving family who will encourage you and be encouraged by you.

If you have done the above encourage all those who have made it possible and please tell me by writing to : –

Gary Armstrong
c/o P.O. BOX 17
Chichester, PO20 6YB
England

It is my desire that those reading this book would see me as an ordinary Christian. If you read and are left pondering about me then this has been a waste of time. But if you are left pondering about the Christ who saved me, then it has been worthy of the time, but more importantly, worthy of the God whom I love, adore, and serve. He who is able to raise from the ashes of despair a monument of grace, He who is able to transform stumbling stones into stepping stones, He who is able to produce wells of joy having used the spade of affliction, He who has not come to call the righteous but sinners to repentance – called me and is still calling – without discrimination the whosoever who **will**. Will you come? If He is able to take this poor lost sinner, lift him from the miry clay and set him free, He will surely do no less for you. Whether it be trouble, whether it be sorrow, whether it be financial disaster, whether it be emptiness, Christ is able to turn your blunders into blessing if you will but let him.

*"In my distress I cried unto the Lord and He delivered me".*